No Soft Incense:

Barbara Pym
and the Church

D1082741

Edited by Hazel K. Bell

Barbara Pym Society

Published by Anna Brown Associates
14 Flag Court, Courteney Terrace, Hove, BN3 2WG
in association with the Barbara Pym Society
St Hilda's College, Oxford 2004

ISBN 0-9543316-6-4

Index compiled by Hazel K. Bell
Designed and typeset by HKB Typesetting
139 the Ryde
Hatfield, Herts, AL9 5DP

Printed by Lynx dpm Limited, Chalgrove, Oxfordshire

Barbara Pym: 1913–1980

"I cannot see what flowers are at my feet", said Julian softly.
Nor what soft incense hangs upon the boughs, I continued to myself ...
"That's Keats, isn't it?" I asked ... "I always think *Nor What Soft Incense* would be a splendid title for a novel."

– from *Excellent Women* by Barbara Pym, Chapter 22.

Contents

Foreword

There are some seventy-five clergymen in the work of Barbara Pym, which averages out at 5.76 a novel. Quite what 0.76 of a clergyman might be like would, I think, have amused her. What could have marked the man down? Pomposity? Snobbery? Absence of humour? Or perhaps the simple thoughtlessness of having a wife. 'Just imagine, a married curate,' says Harriet "in disgust" in *Some Tame Gazelle*. A young married clergyman simply isn't playing fair.

The churches themselves are sturdy Victorian buildings, Anglo-Catholic in temperament, filled with the lingering smell of incense and lit by low-wattage lamps and a few guttering candles. They offer the timeless reassurance of daily Holy Communion, Sung Eucharist on Sundays, Confession and the Reservation of the Blessed Sacrament. The clergy who officiate might be kindly, hapless, holy fools, or vain beyond measure; but they are invariably, as Kate Charles points out, 'at ease with ladies.' It is how these women deal with the uniquely clerical mixture of pride and incompetence that makes up much of Pym's humour. Miss Morrow, in *Crampton Hodnet*, for example, finds herself being proposed to by a curate who cannot actually remember her Christian name:

'Oh, Miss Morrow – Janie,' he burst out suddenly.

'My name isn't Janie.'

'Well, it's something beginning with J,' he said impatiently. It was annoying to be held up by such a triviality. What did it matter what her name was at this moment?

Certainly, Barbara Pym knew such a world of expectation and anxiety intimately, and the pages that follow celebrate the churches, clergymen, and congregations that populate her novels. They should provide equal pleasure to Pym *aficionados*, the disinterested reader, and the academic (not that these are mutually exclusive!). If you require elegant literary criticism, with references to Bakhtin and Simone Weil, then there are essays by David Cockerell, Eleonore Biber and Judy McInnes; if you seek biographical details of the churches Barbara Pym attended, wish to enrich your understanding of Roman Catholicism, or need to consult a glossary of her fictional clergy then Robert Smith, Joy Grant, and Gerard Irvine are ready and waiting; and for detailed analysis of excellent women, class distinction, and clergy wives then Kate Charles, Tim Burnett, and Triona Adams will guide you; and if you would like the tender testimony of a father fan then there are no less than three humane and illuminating essays by Gabriel Myers.

It is good that the clergy themselves are well represented in this volume, because Pym herself was so admiringly critical of them. I think she was intrigued and puzzled, loving and also slightly suspicious, as if she could not always believe in their intentions. Were they, perhaps, at times too good to be true? Implicit at the heart of her novels lies one crucial question; what do the clergy actually do with their time? Of course they pray, and this is of vital importance; they officiate at services, reassuring their congregation with the consolation of the sacraments and the confidence of the pulpit; they open fetes, bazaars, jumble sales and tombolas; they tend to the sick and dying; but can this really be all? They are forever telling their parishioners that they are rushed off their feet; but can this be accurate? If so, then why are they seen holding ping-pong bats and quoting inappropriate passages from Keats or Milton? How do they find time to woo unsuitable women, or to enjoy light Sunday suppers in the company of spinsters who worry about birds, woodworm and the Jesuits?

Pym understands the way in which many clergymen convey a lifestyle so hectic that they cannot quite cope and need help: serious, regular, help, preferably from adoring and 'excellent' women who will be there to cook, type, arrange flowers, wash albs, and wrap up presents at Christmas. They need ladies to see to their cassocks, mend their socks, cook boiled chicken, and type up their sermons for collection in some august future volume.

Sometimes this is genuine haplessness. Nicholas Cleveland in *Jane and Prudence* is a vague, kindly, holy fool whose principal enthusiasm rests in animal-shaped soaps. But Tom Dagnall in *A Few Green Leaves* and David Lydell in *Quartet in Autumn* are rather more calculating, as Letty realizes while eating a *Poulet Niçoise* that she is sure the Vicar has sampled many times before:

Had David Lydell gone all round the village sampling the cooking of the unattached women before deciding which one to settle with?

Some of the ladies are very much on to this hapless little game, realizing that any future drudgery is not so much divine as 'standing at the sink with aching back and hands plunged into the washing up water' or running 'up and down stairs with glasses of hot milk and poached eggs'. Others, however, are still filled with the somewhat questionable hope that marriage to a clergyman might offer nothing less than an earthly glimpse of the paradise to come.

In any other author such ironic observational humour could be crude and unforgiving, but Barbara Pym's writing contains both gentleness and a startling lack of ego that both tempers and blesses the acuity of her observation. It celebrates all that is best of Christian wisdom and generosity; hopeful without being trite, loving without being naïve, comic without being cruel. It is both reassuring and realistic, born of the knowledge of the need for simple pleasures, well-spaced treats, and the advantages of a generous heart. In her work, and also through this book, comes an awareness that we are all, ultimately, little more than holy fools, caught in the divine comedy of life; a comedy which can move almost effortlessly from the remorselessly trivial to the ineffably profound. Our task is simply to work out which is which.

James Runcie

What relevance does the Church of Barbara Pym have to the world and Church of today?

The Revd. David Cockerell

Like many British institutions, the Church of England has changed markedly in the last forty years or so, and is still changing, perhaps more rapidly than at any other time in its history. Some people may regret this change, and others welcome it; but in any case it raises for us the question as to why we should read a novelist whose portrait of the church is in many ways that of something now gone. Is this really any more than an exercise in nostalgia?

Let me begin with my first and last excursus into theology, in order to make my own theological presupposition clear. For example, the teaching of Jesus and the development of early Christianity have to be seen in the context of a range of religious ideas which were jostling for prominence within Judaism at that time; for it seems to me that the God of the Bible and of the church's tradition is a God of change, who is constantly on the move, and constantly calling his people onwards to new challenges in new ages. We see at the moment a scholarly emphasis upon the complexity of Biblical religion, seen nowadays not so much as the tidy ordered religious system of an older generation of German scholars but more as a blooming, buzzing profusion of ideas and beliefs. Religion which is creative and alive is always about change, and the dangers of idealising ideas and practices from a past, particularly a supposed 'golden age', were certainly already present in Biblical times.

The church forms an important part of the background of Barbara Pym's novels. Probably few English novelists of the postwar period have described it so sympathetically and humorously. Her interest in the church is signalled on the very first page of her first published book, *Some Tame Gazelle,* which appeared in 1950.

Its style, acute observation of character, and a gentle comedy which delights in the absurdity of human behaviour, is often revealed through a careful attention to small details. If her books are about the search for something to live by, then that is mediated not through systems and philosophies but through the small, apparently mundane affairs of everyday human life. The emotional and spiritual thrust of the novels rests in the recognition that they are neither small nor mundane for those whose lives they are. An American scholar, Michael Cotsell, has commented:[1]

> Pym's novels are apparently 'not about anything', or not very much, and are full of conversation which is amusing if not always witty. But in being about nothing, Pym's novels also affirm something, the little gestures and commitments, the feelings and doings of the ordinary world.

In this way, that world is redeemed, transfigured into the material out of which we fashion for ourselves a world of moral and spiritual meaning and purpose. If along the way we come to realise that the world is also comic and even absurd, then we also acknowledge the true nature of that purpose.

Barbara Pym was a practising Anglican, attracted to the Anglo-Catholicism of the London churches she attended; and a characteristic Pym creation, partly self-portrait, is Mildred Lathbury, the central character of Pym's second and perhaps best-known novel, *Excellent Women* (1952). Mildred is a conventional church-going spinster whose quiet and undemanding world of Anglo-Catholic religion, PCCs and church fetes is suddenly disturbed by the arrival of her new neighbours, Rocky and Helena Napier. Mildred finds herself caught up in the headstrong and (by her standards) unconventional world of the dashing ex-Naval captain Rocky, and Helena, who is an anthropologist. Through Helena, Mildred meets Everard Bone, another anthropologist with whom Helena is preparing a learned paper, and to whom Mildred finds herself drawn.

During the 1950s Pym published a further four novels, notably *A Glass of Blessings* (1958), with its title from George Herbert reflecting her love of seventeenth-century English verse, which often forms a sort of emotional commentary to her books. Again it is worth pausing to sample its opening:

> I suppose it must have been the shock of hearing the telephone ring, apparently in the church, that made me turn my head and see Piers Longridge in one of the side aisles behind me. It sounded shrill and particularly urgent against the music of the organ, and it was probably because I had never before heard a telephone ringing in church that my thoughts were immediately distracted, so that I found myself wondering where it could be and whether anyone would answer it. I imagined the little bent woman in the peacock blue hat who acted as verger going into the vestry and picking up the receiver gingerly, if only to put an end to the loud unsuitable ringing. She might say that Father Thames was engaged at the moment or not available; but surely the caller ought to have known that, for it was St Luke's day, the patronal festival of the church, and this lunchtime Mass was one of the services held for people who worked in the offices nearby or perhaps for the idle ones like myself who had been too lazy to get up for an earlier service.

Notice how quickly and deftly the world which the novel will occupy is established and described in its opening paragraph. At the centre of this is a contrast: the inconsiderate telephone bell with its 'loud unsuitable' ringing on the one hand; and, the sanctuary bell on the other. The latter stands for the comfort and security of Wilmet's familiar world of Anglo-Catholic devotion; the former represents the shrill challenge of modernity, the impersonality of the machine, rudely threatening to displace the other. This is the conflict in which Wilmet, like Mildred Lathbury, will find herself caught up: on the one hand the conventional, if dull, world represented by the church and her unexciting husband, Rodney; on the other a world of different and more dashing possibilities suggested by another in Pym's cast of tantalising but inaccessible men, Piers Longridge. Piers is gay, and Wilmet's rival for his affections is a man called Keith. So Wilmet comes to see that the 'glass of blessings' is given by God to those whom he chooses, and that we cannot therefore take them for granted or look down on those whom we feel lack them. They are mediated in and through the small things, and our spiritual task is to see our lives, however mundane, they may seem, as a 'glass of blessings'. To quote George Herbert:

When God at first made Man
Having a glass of blessings standing by;
Let us (said he) pour on him all we can:
Let the world's riches, which dispersed lie,
Contract into a span.

Although Barbara Pym had no anthropological qualification to work at the International African Institute on its journal, *Africa*, it is easy to see that the outlook of the anthropologist, based upon a cool and detached observation of the details of human behaviour, was in tune with her understanding of the task of the novelist. As Rocky Napier comments to Mildred, when they are to go to hear Helena and Everard's paper at the 'Learned Society':

"Yes, Miss Lathbury, you and I will sit at the back and observe the anthropologists ... They study mankind and we will study them."

That very much sums up what Pym was doing for much of her life; she once suggested that the novelist might be to our society something of what the social anthropologist is to 'primitive' societies. But there was a deeper and more important acquisition from anthropology in Pym's understanding of the place of ritual in human life. Ritual does not merely reflect or express our search for value or purpose in life, our 'something to live by'; it actually makes it possible. Ritual is necessary as the means by which public meaning and purpose are given to individual and private lives. Barbara Pym's novels describe the ritual systems through which people create such meaning and purpose in our society, just as the anthropologist describes such systens in 'primitive' society.

The most important of these ritual-systems is provided through religion, and many of the novels are set against the ritually-rich world of Anglo-Catholicism – and not only the explicit ritual of the liturgy, but also, and for many of Pym's characters more importantly, the rituals of church cleaning and decorating, tea-making and bazaar organising, with their patterns and hierarchies whose infringements produce confusion and castigation. Pym drew humour from these situations, but the humour is never sarcastic or dismissive because behind the comedy is a recognition of an underlying seriousness, at least to the individuals involved.

"Well, well, here we all are," said Julian in a rather more clerical tone than usual. "It's very good of you all to come along and help and I'm especially grateful to all those who have brought flowers. Lady Farmer," he mentioned the only titled member remaining in our congregation, "has most kindly sent these magnificent lilies from her country home."
There was a pause.
"Is he going to say a prayer?" whispered Sister Blatt to me, and as nobody broke the silence I bent my head suitably and waited. But the words Julian spoke were

not a prayer but a gay greeting to Allegra Gray, who came in through the door at that moment.

"Ah, here you are, now we can start."

"Well, really, were we just waiting for *her*?" mumbled Sister Blatt. "We've been decorating for years – long before Mrs Gray came."

"Well, she is a newcomer, perhaps Father Malory thought it more polite to wait for her. I dare say he will help her."

"Father Malory help with the decorating! These men will never do anything. I expect they'll slink off and have a cup of coffee once the work starts." (EW 110)

The men are typically seen as ineffectual and time-wasting. This emphasis upon the ethical and social importance of ritual needs to be borne in mind if we are to avoid the complaint that Pym is only concerned with externalities in her treatment of religion. It is true that we have to look hard within her books for explicit examples of theological debate or spiritual struggle – yet there is a kind of struggle going on all the time, the struggle to find something to live by in an age when the older sureties are breaking down. There is certainly no room here for a disembodied 'spirituality' which can carry on without such contingencies, and ignoring these means ignoring the reality which incarnates the faith in the lives of its followers. When Mildred comes close to despair, she goes to church and tries to pray, but is disturbed by the church cleaner who thinks that she must be ill:

I opened the door rather timidly and went in. I was relieved to see that there was nobody else there and I sat down hopelessly and waited, I did not know what for. I did not feel that I could organise my thoughts but I hoped that if I sat there quietly I might draw some comfort from the atmosphere. Centuries of devotion leave their mark in a place, I knew, but then I remembered that it was barely seventy years since St Mary's had been built; it seemed so bright and new and there were no canopied tombs of great families, no weeping cherubs, no urns, no worn inscriptions on the floor. Instead I could only read the brass tablets to past vicars and benefactors or contemplate the ugly stained glass of the east window. And yet, I thought after a while, wasn't the atmosphere of good Victorian piety as comforting as any other? Ought I not to be as much consoled by the thought of our first vicar, Father Busby – Henry Bertram Busby and Maud Elizabeth, his wife – as by any seventeenth century divine? I was half unconscious of my surroundings now and started when I heard a voice calling my name.

"Miss Lathbury! Miss Lathbury!"

I looked up almost guiltily as if I had been doing something disgraceful and saw Miss Statham creeping towards me. She held a polishing-cloth and a tin of Brasso in her hand.

"You were sitting so still, I thought perhaps you'd had a turn."(EW p.155)

The message is clear: what is real in the church lies in such contingencies as cleaning and decorating, whilst the prayer, or the attempt to pray, is something rather self-conscious, a suggestion of something not quite right. Once again it is the apparently trivial which is what shapes and carries the faithful.

For Pym, as a lay anthropologist, religion was to do with ritual, rather than with theology. She implicitly challenges the dichotomy between the material and the spiritual: starkly put, is it prayer or Brasso, or Brasso as prayer? Spirituality, in other words, is something which is to be worked at and worked out, in and through the practicalities of everyday life: not only cleaning brasses, but wrestling with the kind of emotional and ethical problems that befall many of her central characters. It is the 'practical divinity' of such seventeenth century Anglican writers as George Herbert, for whose writing Pym had a particular affection:

Teach me, my God and king, in all things thee to see
And what I do in anything, to do it as for thee

A servant with this clause makes drudgery divine
Who sweeps a room as for thy laws makes that and th'action fine

Notice too, that this is very much a lay perspective of the church and its faith, and clergy are often seen as ineffectual, as we saw in the passage quoted above about Father Julian: 'These men will never do anything. I expect they'll slink off and have a cup of coffee once the real work starts'. More bleakly, to move on to *Quartet in Autumn*, when Edwin and Father Gellibrand stumble across the sick – indeed dying – Marcia, Gellibrand is shown as helpless and can do nothing except make his excuses and leave. It is Edwin who now makes the practical arrangements. In the same novel, when Marcia and Letty retire, the manager who makes the speech at their farewell party says that 'the point about Miss Crowe and Miss Ivory is that nobody knows, or has ever known exactly what it is they do'. A sad, and even rather pathetic epitaph on a working life, we might think. But the point is that we can no more expect this male manager to understand what Miss Crowe or Miss Ivory do than Father Julian understands what the excellent women in his church do, or as we will see Tom in AFGL understand what Miss Lee and Miss Grundy do. 'I expect they'll slink off for a cup of coffee once the real work starts'. It is (let the reader understand) the Brasso tin or the polish or calling the ambulance for a dying woman that is the 'real work'.

The church and its faith is so often defined and described by clergy, theologians and philosophers. Through their definitions and descriptions they define and affirm power not only for those descriptions but for themselves. Barbara Pym's voice is important not least because she challenges those descriptions on behalf of those of whom 'nobody knows, or has ever known, exactly what it is they do', but who in fact do everything. We are reminded of Jesus's teaching in parables, not merely as entertaining visual aids, but because this is how God is best known: in, and through, story. God is, if we like, a storied god, and the stories are often about ordinary people. 'The Kingdom of God is like a woman who ..., a man who ..., a farmer who ...', and the anonymity of these characters is part of the point of the parable, because in being anonymous they are stripped of identity to stand alongside those of whom nobody knows exactly what it is that they do.

I will not go into the circumstances of Barbara Pym's literary rejection and illness. But I have already mentioned the first of her 'rediscovery' novels, *Quartet in Autumn*, which was shortlisted for the Booker Prize in 1977.

This superbly crafted novel is about four people, two men and two women, moving into retirement from an office which is itself being closed down. Letty Crowe is a recognisable Pym creation: a sensible, conventional spinster whose plans to retire to the country to live with her old friend Marjorie are upset when Marjorie becomes engaged to the local vicar. The other woman in the quartet, Marcia Ivory, is a quite new, and brilliant, creation: an eccentric who lives increasingly reclusively in the house she shared with her mother until the latter's death. Her greatest interests are her mastectomy and her infatuation with her surgeon, the significantly named Mr Strong. We watch Marcia move from eccentricity to madness, a movement which is deftly but starkly portrayed, and which hints at darker aspects of Pym's own struggle with illness and rejection. If the 'sensible' Letty is the more obvious Pym character, the one she kept on show to her friends and colleagues, Marcia suggests a more worried and worrying side to her, an altogether more complex and troubled person. She hoards milk-bottles, cans of food (unopened, for she rarely eats anything), paper bags and pieces of string, and her days pass quickly in classifying and re-classifying them – obsessive behaviour which parodies the rituals which gave meaning and purpose to characters in the earlier novels. Cancer-suffering and anorexic, she finally collapses after a visit to the affluent suburb where Mr Strong lives, and she dies in hospital, her life finally consummated through death in the gentle, if slightly impersonal, care of Mr Strong.

We notice that the church no longer provides a background or point of reference. Edwin, the only churchgoer of the four, is viewed as an object of amusement and even of pity, as he rushes from one church to another, apparently engaged on a restless search for ... what? As we have seen, when Edwin and his parish priest Father Gellibrand stumble across Marcia after she has collapsed at home, Gellibrand only feels helpless and is glad to get away. For Marcia, the aptly-named Mr Strong is 'God', and her visits to his home – which she gazes at in awe but never enters – have the quality of pilgrimage. There is a conscious (or semi-conscious) return to the opening of *A Glass of Blessings;* but here in QIA the tone and the message are very different:

> Tonight, being the 18th October and St Luke's Day, [Edwin] was hoping to find an evening Mass somewhere. The lunchtime churches had yielded nothing, a sad contrast to the days when Father Thames and Father Bode had attracted a crowd of office workers. Edwin also thought regretfully of another church where he had often gone in the past, which would have provided a splendid service, but that church was no more. A scandal in the early fifties – Edwin remembered it well – had put an end to the splendid services, the congregation had fallen away and in the end the church had been closed as redundant. An office block now stood on the spot where the air had once been filled with incense. It was a sad story, but the upshot of it was that there would be no St Luke's day evening Mass *there*. Luke, the beloved physician. (QA p.166).

A sad story indeed; and so, with the reference to St Luke which points back to the earlier book, Barbara Pym modulates to the real focus of modern religion, medicine and the powerful, capable figure of the doctor. So Edwin's intention of going to church on St Luke's day has to be 'given up', leaving us with the question: has the church itself 'given up'? Certainly, there is a note of regret and sadness in this passage, a looking back to a church which was no more, a church in which Pym herself could have found solace.

It is easy to read here, as I have suggested, a note of regret for a church, and a way of being the church, which had already largely disappeared by the time QIA was written. It would be easy to see simply nostalgia for a past which no longer exists. But perhaps what we have here is really something braver: a recognition that the church belongs – and continues to belong – in an ever-new, ever-changing world. Just as in *A Glass of Blessings* the sanctuary bell is drowned out by the telephone bell, so here the church building itself has been replaced by an office block. If the values and ideals of the Christian church are to survive, they now have to do so in a world which is far more challenging, and perhaps more painful, than that earlier comfort and security of lunchtime Masses.

Through the characters of Edwin and the ineffectual Father Gellibrand, Pym shows us that this world, if indeed it ever existed, has gone. It is the lonely and rather sad figure of Edwin who is the nostalgist, and in a novel of self-discovery and self-awareness (perhaps as much for its author as for its characters), Edwin has to discover that the church of his imaginings is no more. A painful discovery, yes. A sad story, certainly. But if QIA is partly about facing the truth about oneself and one's circumstances, then that realization is central for Edwin. Perhaps it was central too for Barbara Pym herself? The church will live in a new world, the world symbolized by the telephone and the office-block; or it, too, will die.

The bleakness of this fine, and at times funny, book lies in its undermining of the very features which had given point and purpose to life in the earlier novels. Indeed, it begins to look as if their comfort was illusory and the only true, non-delusory prospect is, after all, the radical freedom found by Marcia through madness and death. There is, though, a hint of a more positive possibility at the end of the novel, when we learn that Marjorie has broken her engagement to the vicar and assumes that Letty will, after all, go to live with her. But, after Marcia's death, Letty realises that she does not have to do what is expected of her by others, that she can shape her own destiny – as, by implication, Marcia had done. She acquires a 'feeling of power', a realisation that she can find purpose in life through the exercise of freewill, of choice. Likewise Norman, who to everyone's surprise (not least his own) has inherited Marcia's house, realises that he can actually choose whether to sell it or keep it. He sees 'that he had the power to influence the lives of people' like Marcia's former neighbours – as Letty sees that she can influence the life of Marjorie and choose *not* to go to live with her. With choice, with influence over the destinies of others, comes power and a sense of liberation. The search for something to live by is now personalised and internalised in the notion of 'choice' and no longer rests on the public world of ritual. But where does that power lead? That is the question addressed in Pym's next book, *The Sweet Dove Died.*

This novel is unique in Barbara Pym's output in having no church or anthropological background. The public world of ritual which they suggested has been stuffed away completely. The book tells the story of Leonora Eyre, a wealthy, snobbish and fastidious woman in later middle age, and her complicated and obsessive relationship with James, a much younger man who is being trained in the antiques trade by his uncle, Humphrey. The story charts a woman's infatuation with a much younger man, dwelling on the predatory and ultimately destructive nature of this relationship. Leonora, who craves perfection in everything, cannot tolerate rivals, and becomes irrationally jealous when she discovers that James has started a relationship with Phoebe, a girl he meets at a party. James' affection for Phoebe is, though, half-hearted, and it transpires that her more serious rival is the manipulative Ned, a gay American research student who actually understands Leonora and the nature of her relationship with James better than she does herself because, of course, they are of the same type. Leonora is finally brought to see that as an ageing woman she has nothing to offer James; she ends up alone and lonely, the victim of her own craving for purity and perfection, and veering, like Marcia, painfully close to obsession and madness.

Like Letty and Norman, Leonora attempts to exercise choice through control over those around her; but it leads not to liberation but to destruction. We need, after all, something larger to live by than a route through life which is based upon individual choices and projects. But where is that to come from? Barbara Pym's final answer is, despite her attempts to free her characters (and herself) from it, the church. In her last novel, written in her final months and published posthumously, Pym returns to the world of the rural village and recognisable Pym casting of anthropologist, rector, and excellent women. At first sight this might seem a disappointment: have we really come all this way to return, full circle, to the world of *Some Tame Gazelle*? The central character of *A Few Green Leaves* is Emma Howick, a young anthropologist researching village life, but distracted by the attentions of Graham Pettifer, her student days lover who is now a successful academic sociologist and television pundit; and Tom, the rector, who lives a curious half-life of marginalisation and pointlessness. Here we have the now familiar contrast between the worlds of anthropologist and doctor (science, the new), and the church (the old). Pym notes that 'whereas the doctor's surgery was always full, the rector's study was empty – never any queues there'. Medicine has, as in *Quartet in Autumn*, replaced religion as the focus for people's spiritual needs, and even the rector's sister goes to the doctor rather than to church when she feels 'low'. Symbolically too, the wife of the ambitious young doctor wants to live in the rectory, thereby appropriating its status, and she suggests to Tom that perhaps he should live somewhere smaller and (by implication) more appropriate to his changed role in the community. Emma views him as 'poor Tom', an ineffectual and rather pathetic figure; but comes through the novel to see that he represents more enduring and deeper values, and that 'relevance' might not after all be everything. Ultimately it is to Tom that she turns for love, rather than the more flamboyant (but superficial) figure of Graham Pettifer.

This final book returns, then, to the struggle between the worlds represented by the church and by modernity. It re-affirms Pym's ultimate conviction that the former offers qualities and values which, albeit unfashionable and rarely explicit, are nevertheless of real and lasting value. At the end of the day it is the world of faithfulness represented by the 'excellent women' Miss Lee and Miss Grundy that offers a real, if imperfect prospect of something to live by. Tom, in a mood of self doubt, comes across these women cleaning the church:

> He found himself speculating on whether Miss Lee had ever had 'doubts'; if, when rubbing the brass head of the eagle lectern, she had ever wondered whether the whole business wasn't an elaborate fiction and asked herself what she was doing here, Sunday after Sunday and even some weekdays, subscribing to something she wasn't sure about. Could he possibly ask her? he wondered, his eyes roving round the church and finding proof of her industry wherever he looked. But it was while he was doing this that his glance fell on the lectern, the brazen bird of his imaginings, and he suddenly realised that it was not made of brass at all but of wood. It was an oak lectern made, according to an inaccurate local legend, from a tree on the the de Tankerville estate. He must have been remembering some other lectern, probably the one in the church of his childhood. How could he have been so forgetful and unobservant! So now the question he put to Miss Lee was nothing to do with faith or lack of it but something much simpler. 'Do you ever wish we had a brass lectern?' he asked. 'As they have in some other churches?'
> 'Oh no, rector,' she answered. 'I love that old wooden bird, and I love polishing it. A brass one may look more brilliant, but wood can be very rewarding, you know, and I think I can flatter myself that nobody can get a better polish on it than I do.'
> Tom turned aside, humbled by her words. It was almost an idea for a sermon, what she said about brass looking more brilliant but wood being very rewarding. Of course Miss Lee never had doubts! And if she ever had, she was much too well-bred ever to dream of troubling the rector with such a thing. (pp. 179-80)

The French philosopher Simone Weil may seem at first sight to have little in common with the English novelist Barbara Pym; and no doubt were Miss Pym with us today she would make delicious humour out of any comparison I might draw. But they were both somewhat idiosyncratic Christians who shared a love for the poetry of George Herbert. Weil's conversion to Christianity was much influenced by her meditation on, and learning by heart. Herbert's great poem 'Love':

Love bade me welcome: yet my soul drew back,
Guiltie of dust and sinne.
But quick-eyed Love, observing me grow slack
From my first entrance in,
Drew nearer to me, sweetly questioning,
If I lack'd any thing.

Weil would be drawn by the platonism of this beautiful poem, as well as by its emphasis upon the inadequacy of human beings to approach the divine, and the element of struggle involved, which corresponded closely with her feelings at this time. Weil described 'Love' to her friend and biographer Simone Petrement as 'the most beautiful poem in the world'; and it is interesting to speculate that she may subconsciously have recognised a deeper affinity with its author.[2] Both were people who had deliberately turned their backs on a comfortable and affluent bourgeois background in favour of a life of some austerity and simplicity. Both died relatively young – Herbert at 40 and Weil at 33; and if it be replied that people died younger anyhow in Herbert's day, we can point out that both were people who consciously chose, despite physical weakness, a life-style of relative discomfort and asceticism. Furthermore, in both cases their spiritual journeys involved struggle, what R.S. Thomas described in Herbert's verse as 'encounter and argument'.

Both had, too, an interest in the lives of working people: Herbert's concern for the lives and work of farmers and agricultural affairs. Weil too, though for rather different reasons, was fascinated by the lives of workers, and obsessed with a desire to identify with them through sharing their lives as fully as she could: hence her ill-judged experiment of working in a car factory. Ill-judged or not, though, she recognised that Herbert's love required incarnation through active participation in the lives of the poorest and most exploited of workers. Real understanding, what she called 'attention', could only come through such participation, even if it meant struggle and physical and emotional pain. As she wrote of her Renault experience, 'I came near to being broken'; but it was only through that sense of brokenness, what she called 'affliction', that she could come to goodness and truth: as she wrote later, 'the sense of human misery is a pre-condition of justice and love'. And this led directly to her understanding of Christianity: that God's Kingdom belongs to the room-sweepers and the factory-workers; as she wrote, 'Christianity is pre-eminently the religion of slaves, that slaves cannot help belonging to it, and I among others'.

What has this to do with the world of Barbara Pym? There may seem little in common between them. Pym had little interest, in her novels, in poor or working people: the world she describes is largely one of affluence and comfort, and this may indeed have accounted in part for her loss of appeal in the 1960s with its vogue for working-class realism.

As yet there is in her writing a different kind of concern for the marginalised, as in her remarkably frank (for its time) portrayal of gay characters, and, as I have said, those whose position is so obscure that no-one knows what it is that they do – or indeed, perhaps that they exist. These are the anonymous ones, the room-sweepers, the factory workers and slaves. If there is nothing in Pym of the somewhat self-indulgent gestures which Weil at her most infuriating could indulge in – and certainly nothing of her left-wing politics – it is not unreasonable to see at work the same Christian impulse, even if the form and the expression is rather different.

Again, in Weil and Herbert we see something of an emphasis on what Weil called 'affliction': and I think we can see something of this too in Barbara Pym. Her ironic description of Letty and Marcia may well have expressed something of her own sense of being ignored and neglected as she confronted the bleakest fate to befall a writer: facing her own literary oblivion. Suppose this was to be her own epitaph?

Did this, combined with her illness, lead her to write out of her own deepest fears and anxieties in the figures of Marcia Ivory and Leonora Eyre? Are these characters in one sense Pym's own act of spiritual defiance? We are reminded again of Herbert, whose spiritual journey involved, according to R.S. Thomas, 'dialogue, encounter, confrontation', something summed up in his poem 'The Collar':

I struck the board and cry'd No more,
I will abroad

Like Jonah, the poet struggles to escape from God and his purposes; but the attempt is of course futile:

But as I raved and grew more fierce and wilde
At every word,
Me thoughts I heard one calling, Childe!
And I replied, My Lord.

The journey abroad leads only to the 'fierce and wilde' veering towards the madness of Marcia and Leonora: is this Barbara Pym's way of echoing Simone Weil's 'I came near to being broken'? Perhaps the resolution of the final novel, with its re-affirmation of the church and its values, could emerge only out of that sense of brokenness – though even here, Tom, like Edwin, has to leave behind the church of his imaginings before he can hear the voice mediated through Miss Lee and Miss Grundy:

Me thought I heard one calling, Childe!
And I replied, My Lord.

References

1. Cotsell, Michael. *Barbara Pym*. London: Macmillan, 1989.
2. Petremont, Simone. *Simone Weil: a life*. 1976

Exploring London churches
with Barbara Pym

Robert Smith

Barbara was brought up as and remained throughout her life a member of the Church of England, and to her all its churches were places of devotion and interest. When after War service and her mother's death she came to live with her sister in London, and 'already well into churchgoing' as her sister has written,[1] she became a regular worshipper at:

1. St Gabriel's Church, Warwick Square, Pimlico

This mid-Victorian (1854) near-Gothic church became dear to Barbara, and is dear to us because it is St Mary's, the church which with its vicar, curates, jumble sales and boys' club plays an important part in *Excellent Women*. In Barbara's day the services were somewhat 'middle of the road' and so Barbara – daughter of Oxford and a former member of the God-fearing Royal Navy – was soon 'wanting something higher with more ritual'.[2] Then, at about this time her employers, the International African Institute, moved their offices to Fetter Lane and thus brought her within an easy walk at lunchtime to:

2. St Alban's the Martyr, Holborn

This famous church, 'one of the strongest of the works' of the architect William Butterfield, was a centre for the practice in London of the 'full Anglo-Catholic faith'. Destroyed by German bombs in 1941, it was the temporary church amid the ruins to which Barbara found her way in 1955 and where she read the parish magazine in the porch: 'Don't quite like to smoke or read Proust';[3] and where Mildred met Everard Bone.[4]

In 1949 Barbara and Hilary moved to Barnes, the background to *Less Than Angels,* and here Barbara joined the Parochial Church Council of:

3. St Michael and All Angels Church, Barnes Bridge

A rather dull late 19th-century building which provided the background to services in a sound and advanced Western Catholic tradition.

About this time I returned from Africa and found a flat reasonably convenient for commuting into Central London. Then began a period during which Barbara and I were meeting around London fairly regularly. We soon found a mutual interest in churches, especially Anglican churches. It was not the architecture which came first with us but an exploration of the different atmospheres and backgrounds which we found, usually the 'higher' the better, and the differing congregation. First, let me refer to:

4. St Mary's Aldermary, Queen Victoria Street, City of London

This was – and I suppose still is — a City Guild church, that is, without a district parish life. Here the priest was Father Freddy Hood, known to us both from his years in Oxford as principal of Pusey House where the colourful services based strictly on the ritual prescriptions of Adrian Fortescue [5] rivalled the quieter Prayer Book services in the college chapels. We recalled Fr. Hood's invitations in Oxford to 'Sherry and compline'. I recall also that it was in this church that we heard a telephone bell ringing in the vestry, speculation about which provided the opening pages for *A Glass of Blessings.*

Next there is:

5. St Mary-Le-Strand

This mediaeval church was rebuilt in the 18th century by James Gibbs and is described by Nikolaus Pevsner as like 'a casket one can handle with one's hands'. Barbara and I visited it one 30th January, the anniversary of the beheading of King Charles I, saint and martyr, whose shrine is in the church and whose martyrdom was a subject that morning of a sermon by the Abbot of Nushdom.

Moving west to:

6. St James's Church, Piccadilly

A fashionable 'middle stump' church before the war, after which the late 17th-century building (by Wren) had to be largely rebuilt. Barbara and I visited it in its transitory period under Dean Baddeley who once announced at Mattins, 'Here endeth that perfectly lovely Second Lesson'.

Then to Notting Hill, and to:

7. All Saints Church, Talbot Road, Notting Hill

This church had suffered from bombing, and like St Alban's it too was a shrine to advanced Anglo-Catholicism. The vicar was the redoubtable Fr. Twisaday, whose likeness as Fr. Thames appears in *A Glass of Blessings*, which also contains a somewhat evocative clergy-house. Our visits there led us to:

8. Holy Innocents Church, Paddenswick Road, Hammersmith

Here we attended the induction as its new vicar of Fr. Sean McAteer, formerly curate of All Saints. The induction in *A Glass of Blessings* of the languid and charming Fr. Marius Ransome owes much to this, as also to the next description:

9. St Cyprian's Church, Clarence Gate, Regent's Park

A modern church (1903) of whose interior Pevsner writes: 'There is no reason for the excesses of praise lavished on John Comper's church furnishings by those who confound aesthetic with religious emotions'. Here we again attended an induction of a new vicar. While we entered Barbara memorised a clerical conversation which we overheard:

> 'Are you robing, Father?' ...
> 'Rather!' came the enthusiastic answer ... And I saw that they were both carrying small suitcases, from which I imagined crushed cottas being taken out. [6]

We also visited:

10. St Augustine's Church, Kilburn

A cathedral-like church in North London which became Neville Forbes's church in *No Fond Return of Love*

11. St John the Divine, Richmond, Surrey

Well-known to us both, and memorable to Barbara for its American curate

Finally, sadly:

12. St Lawrence the Martyr, Queen's Park, Brondesbury

This was the parish church of which Barbara and Hilary, after their move from Barnes, became loyal and zealous members. They became members of the Church Council and supporters of parish activities. Members of the congregation became familiar figures, and especially the hard-working organist whom they privately christened 'Bear', and who was transmuted into Bill Coleman of St Luke's, Fr. Thames's church in *A Glass of Blessings*. But before long the congregation began to dwindle, losses being analysed by Babara and Hilary under the headings, 'Rome, Death and Umbrage'. In 1971 the Bishop of London closed the church and it was demolished. By then Barbara had joined Hilary in retirement at Finstock village in Oxfordshire.

References

1. Pym, Hilary Walton. "Barbara Pym in Pimlico." Unpublished manuscript of a talk given at St Gabriel's, Warwick Square, London, 14th February 1996
2. Ibid.
3. Pym, Barbara. *A Very Private Eye*, ed. Hazel Holt & Hilary Pym. London: Macmillan, 1984, p195
4. Pym, Barbara. *Excellent Women*. London: Johnathan Cape, 1952. Chapter 6
5. Fortescue, Adrian. *The Ceremonies of the Roman Rite Described*, 1920 (much of this has been overtaken by the rules of the second Vatican Council.)
6. Pym, Barbara. *A Glass of Blessings*. London: Jonathan Cape, 1958. Chapter 23

A mini-history of Anglo-Catholicism

Kate Charles

In a talk that Hilary Walton gave at St Gabriel's, Pimlico, in 1996, she said:

> What I am leading up to is that when Barbara came to Pimlico she was already well into churchgoing (as you might say), and in London there were plenty of churches to choose from, but her experience had led her, for whatever reason, into wanting something higher, with more ritual, than the ones she was used to – and here was St Gabriel's right on her doorstep. I think it might have been at this point that Barbara bought, at Mowbray's (where else?) a little book called *The Ritual Reason Why* – not only, I might say, for her own enlightenment – and some amusement, because it's written in question-and-answer form – but if she was also going to write about this kind of churchmanship, she must get it right.
>
> She was always a great stickler for accuracy, and I think one of the reasons why clergy enjoy her novels is that she does get things right.

So with the help of *The Ritual Reason Why*, and with reference to the Pym novels themselves, I hope to shed some light on what is today the fairly esoteric world of Anglo-Catholicism, as Barbara Pym knew and experienced it.

What is Anglo-Catholicism? Most people who couldn't define the term itself would recognise the concept of "High" church, as opposed to "Low" church. The Anglo part refers to Anglican, or English, in contrast to Roman Catholic, or the branch of catholicism which receives its authority from the Pope in Rome. Anglo-Catholics consider themselves no less "catholic" than Romans, and would dispute anyone defining the Church of England as a Protestant church.

Historically speaking, the Anglo-Catholic movement found its roots in the middle ages, in the pre-Reformation English Catholic church. By the early 1800s, the Church of England was thoroughly Protestant in character. But in Oxford, in the 1830s, a group of academics began to explore the Church's pre-Reformation history, and the Oxford Movement was born.

What started as a theological exercise began, pretty quickly, to have some practical implications for style of worship. If you believe that the sacraments are more than representative — that, indeed, Christ is present in the consecrated elements of communion — then that influences the way you treat the elements, and indeed the way you construct and fit out your churches. Very soon the followers of the Oxford Movement began to develop a ceremonial style of worship, based on solid scholarship into the worship practices of the pre-Reformation church.

It was all highly controversial in a way which now seems scarcely possible or even believable. There were riots in the streets, and priests went to prison for insisting on practices as unexceptional as putting candlesticks on their altars.

Before too long, a second strand of Anglo-Catholicism emerged, which was less influenced by the pre-Reformation English Church than by the mid-19th century Continental Catholic church. This group adopted Roman-style vestments and practices, and there has always, to the present day, been a certain tension between these two strands.

The hey-day of Anglo-Catholicism was in the 1920s, when the battles had been won and the ceremonial style of worship became fashionable. The vestiges of this carried on well into the 1950s, when Barbara Pym fell under the spell of Anglo-Catholicism and wrote about it in her novels. She obviously had a copy of the famous *Mowbray's Church Guide for Tourists*, which ranked churches according to the availability of what were known as "full Catholic privileges".

The high church vicar of Rowena's country parish speaks to Wilmet in *A Glass of Blessings*: "Ah, St Luke's. You would get full Catholic privileges there," he said rather wistfully.

And in *Less Than Angels* we read:

[the Vicar] was a man in vigorous early middle age who had introduced into the services many features which were new and startling to the congregation. He had been wise enough to do this gradually, so that by the time the church had won the right to have the mysterious letters DSCR after its name in *Mowbray's Church Guide*, most of the congregation were rather proud of themselves for having become High Church almost without knowing it.

So, what do the mysterious letters DSCR mean? D is for Daily celebration of the Holy Communion, S is for Sung Eucharist on Sundays, C is for Confessions, and R is for Reservation of the Blessed Sacrament.

Thus, near the end of *A Glass of Blessings*, Mr Bason tells Wilmet and Rodney how he found his new position:

"An advert in the *Church Times*. One does feel that if one sees something *there* it will be all right, and so it has proved to be. Very convenient all round — A.-C. Church two minutes," he added chirpily. "Reservation."

This light-hearted alphabet, which Barbara Pym would have understood and enjoyed, was prepared by Kate Charles and Eleanore Biber as a guide for the uninitiated.

An Anglo-Catholic A - Z
A is for Anglo-Catholicism
B is for Biretta
C is for Celibacy
D is for Day of Obligation
E is for Evensong and Benediction
F is for Fasting
G is for Going over to Rome
H is for High Mass / Low Mass
I is for Incense
J is for Jingle Bells
K is for Kalendar
L is for Lowder
M is for Mary
N is for Nuns and Monks
0 is for Ornaments
P is for Penitence, Sacrament of (Confession)
Q is for Queens
R is for Ritualism
S is for Servers
T is for Tractarianism
U is for Use
V is for Vestments
W is for Walsingham
X is for the Sacred Monogram
Y is for Year's Mind
Z is for Zucchetto

A strong smell of incense: aspects of Anglo-Catholicism in Barbara Pym's novels

Eleonore Biber

> Eventually I took a bus to St Luke's [...] It was dark and warm inside the church and there was a strong smell of incense. I began to wonder idly whether it was the cheaper brands that smelt stronger, like shag tobacco or inferior tea, but I was sure that Father Thames would have only the very best. I noticed a few professional details, candles burning before the rather brightly coloured statue of our patron saint, a violet stole flung carelessly over one of the confessionals which had curtains of purple brocade. (*AGOB*, 25)

In this paragraph of *A Glass Of Blessings* the world of Anglo-Catholicism is at once deftly established. A number of characteristics of an Anglo-Catholic church are mentioned: votive candles, a statue of a saint, confessionals, and a smell of incense.

Naturally, Wilmet, an Anglo-Catholic, feels quite at home in this sort of church. Catherine in *Less Than Angels* on the other hand is not a regular church-goer. She enters an Anglo-Catholic church which she mistakes for a Roman Catholic church.

> In common with many people who are not regular churchgoers, Catherine sometimes felt the need to enter a church at special times, [...] The one she eventually chose seemed to her just right, with its mysterious dimness pierced by a red light hanging before an altar in a side chapel, and its lingering fragrance of incense. She thought it must be a Roman Catholic church, especially as there was a little table with candles on it, some of which had already been lit, standing in front of a statue. (*LTA*, 190)

A lingering smell of incense is typical of an Anglo-Catholic church. In Mrs Pope's church in *QIA* they do not use incense. Therefore it does not appeal to Edwin who is a staunch Anglo-Catholic.

> [...] the thought of Edwin gave [Letty] a conversational opening and she was able to ask Mrs Pope about his connection with her church.
> 'Oh, he's not a regular member of our congregation – he only comes if there's something special going on,' Mrs Pope said, fiercely scraping a piece of burnt toast. 'We're not nearly high enough for him – no incense, you see.'
> 'No incense?' Again Letty was at a loss. (*QIA* 93)

Poor Letty! She could have asked Edwin, he would have been delighted to explain the trappings of Anglo-Catholicism to her. He would have told her that the Church of England is not monolithic and informed her about the width of its spectrum. He would have talked to her about the concept of 'High Church' as opposed to 'Low Church' and told her about the Oxford Movement and its late phase Anglo-Catholicism.

The term High Church was first used about the end of the 17th century, but there is a continuous High Church tradition in the Church of England throughout the period from the Elizabethan age, when it was largely a response to Puritanism, to our age. The High Church group – giving a 'high' or relatively important place to the episcopate and the sacraments and stressing the continuity with Catholic Christianity – flourished under the Stuarts and came into prominence again with the Oxford Movement. The term Low Church was originally used to denote the liberal group in the Church of England. In the 19th century, however, the liberal group was called Broad Church, constituting a middle-of-the-road movement, whereas the term Low Church came to designate the more evangelical or Protestant wing of the Church of England, giving a 'low' place to the claims of the episcopate, priesthood, and sacraments, and stressing the Protestant rather than the Catholic heritage of the Anglican church, emphasizing biblical faith and personal conversion. Today it is used more broadly to refer to those who prefer informality and immediacy in liturgical celebrations.

High Churchmanship was transformed by the Oxford Movement. It is generally regarded as dating from John Keble's 1833 sermon against the church's being treated as a mere department of the government. The movement's chief object was the defence of the Church of England as a Divine institution. It aimed at spiritual, doctrinal and liturgical renewal by returning to the ideals of the early church and the High Church ideals of the 17th century. The original, largely clerical group, was led by John Keble, John Henry Newman and Edward Bouverie Pusey, all of them members of Oxford colleges, hence Oxford Movement.

Pym seems to have been very interested in the Oxford Movement. In her diaries she records reading various lives of Newman, and like Mildred in *EW*, she found herself going out to dinner unexpectedly, carrying a life of Newman in a string bag. She kept Newman's autobiography and *The Christian Year*, Keble's collection of poems for the church year, in her library.

Belinda in *Some Tame Gazelle*, struggling with ravioli dough, juxtaposes the grandiloquence of Keble's lines from the fourth stanza of his hymn 'New Every Morning is the Love' with her household duties.

The trivial round, the common task,
Would furnish all we ought to ask,
Room to deny ourselves, a road
To bring us daily nearer God.

And here is Belinda, kneading the dough:

The trivial round, the common task – did it furnish *quite* all we needed to ask? Had Keble *really* understood? Sometimes one almost doubted it. Belinda imagined him writing the lines in a Gothic study, panelled in pitch-pine and well dusted that morning by an efficient servant. Not at all the same thing as standing at the sink with aching back and hands plunged into the washing-up water. (*STG*, 227)

The second phase of the Oxford Movement, Anglo-Catholicism, began when the scene moved from the college common room to the parish life of the nation. A second generation of clergy, soon to be known as ritualists, were beginning to make their presence felt in the church.

The average Anglican service tended to be very long and rather dull. The ritualists began to develop a ceremonial style of worship based on pre-Reformation liturgy or mid-19th century Roman-Catholic practices.

Disturbances occurred, priests were prosecuted and even sent to prison for alleged lawlessness. A number of Anglo-Catholic priests devoted their lives to working in the slums of the big cities, where conditions of life were terribly drab and depressing. One of them was Charles Lowder whom Pym mentions in *AGOB*.

When meeting Marius Ransome, the new curate, for the first time, Wilmet recalls Lowder's work in the London slums of the 19th century.

He was certainly very handsome indeed, with his dark wavy hair and large brown eyes. The bones in his face were well defined and his expression serious. I remembered that he had been in the East End and in the worst part of Kensington, and I wondered whether the suffering and poverty he had seen there had left their mark on him, until I realized that it probably wouldn't be like that in these days of the welfare state. I had been thinking of Father Lowder and a hundred years ago. (*AGOB*, 59)

Lowder was called 'Father' because he was like a father to the poor. Later all Anglo-Catholic priests were addressed with 'Father'. Now the title is generally used.

Anglo-Catholicism also fostered a growing interest in church building and decoration. Models were found in the Middle Ages. Therefore churches were mostly built or restored in Neo-Gothic. The altar was the most important feature; reredos, rood screens, coloured glass contributed to the medieval atmosphere.

In *NFRL*, Dulcie, going sleuthing, enters St Ivel's, Neville Forbes' church.

A few lights were on, and through the gilded rood screen she caught glimpses of bright Victorian stained glass and brass candlesticks on the altar. (*NFRL*, 113)

Pym also refers to the Gothic Revival in *EW* when Mildred agrees to have dinner with Everard at his mother's where she finds the atmosphere echoing the contents of her string bag, a biography of Newman. She discerns a 'faintly exotic smell, almost like incense' (*EW*, 136). This imagery of impressions related to an Anglo-Catholic church is taken further when she enters the bathroom 'with much marble and mahogany and a stained-glass window' (*EW*, 137), which triggers off the following associations:

I began to think that it was perhaps suitable that I was carrying a biography of Cardinal Newman in my string bag, and as I washed my hands and tidied my hair I found myself thinking about the Oxford Movement and the architecture associated with it. (*EW*, 137)

After the ritualistic controversy had died down, Anglo-Catholicism went from strength to strength though there were some tensions between the more liberal group and the conservative wing. Anglo-Catholicism was most influential and flamboyant during the 1920s when spectacular Anglo-Catholic congresses were held in London and elsewhere.

Thereafter as an organized party it was weakened by theological differences and disagreements. Meanwhile, however, it had succeeded in changing the texture of the Church of England, raising its standards of worship everywhere.

After the Second World War, the Anglo-Catholics still showed many signs of strength and vigour, as those of Pym's novels written in the fifties show. The decline of Anglo-Catholicism in a secularized society is reflected in *QIA*, written in the seventies. Here is Edwin showing nostalgia for the heyday of Anglo-Catholicism.

> Remembering the emptiness of the church at the service [...] [Edwin] often thought regretfully of those days of the Anglo-Catholic revival in the last century and even the more sympathetic climate of twenty years ago, where Father G., tall and cadaverous in cloak and biretta, would have been rather more in place than in the church of the nineteen seventies where so many priests went in for jeans and long hair. (*QIA*, 16)

The vision has faltered but Anglo-Catholicism is certainly not without followers today and its influence is still apparent.

Pym's portrayal of the Anglo-Catholic milieu is unique. Each of her novels mentions Anglo-Catholicism in some connection.

Father Gerard Irvine, an honorary life member of the Barbara Pym Society, congratulated her on her handling of the churchy aspect of her novels in a letter in 1978.

> Apart from the quiet, subtle, ironic quality which is so widely and rightly admired, may I add how thrilled I am to find a writer who is accurate on Church matters? I know no one who has the feel - let alone the details – of Churchmanship, particularly of High Churchmanship, since Compton Mackenzie's, and after all he was writing of Edwardian Anglo-Catholicism. (*PYM MS* 171, fol. 129)

Father Irvine obviously refers to Mackenzie's *bildungsroman Sinister Street* and his trilogy *The Parson's Progress*.

'The Anglican Church', Janice Rossen contends in her book-length study *The World of Barbara Pym*, 'forms a pervasive background in Pym's novels, as it formed one in her life' (78), a fact that was acknowledged by Pym such as in the BBC broadcast of an interview with Lord David Cecil.

> I have always loved churchgoing. I do like the tradition of the Anglican Church. I do like hymns, churches, buildings, and everything connected with the church.

Churchgoing formed an important part of her childhood and youth. Though from her diaries it seems to have played no major role in her undergraduate life in Oxford, Alison Shell in her essay *Barbara Pym and Ordinary Oxford* states that the Anglo-Catholic revival of the 1920s and 1930s – as prominent in the home of the original Oxford Movement as anywhere – must have had its influence on the ambience of her novels. (10)

When I visited Pym's sister, Hilary Pym, in Finstock some years ago, she told me that Barbara's penchant for Anglo-Catholicism probably began in the war. As a WREN, stationed at Westcliff-on-Sea, she came upon a church which appealed to her.

[...] tonight I found St Alban's, [...] The church was dark and smelled comfortingly of incense – there were little lights burning and a statue of the Virgin Mary. ... I think I must try and go there on Sunday to take away the depressed feeling that the service here gives me. (*AVPE*, 152)

After the war, Pym and her sister moved to Pimlico, London. She chose as her parish that of St Gabriel's, Warwick Square. St Mary's in EW is based on it. In a talk Hilary gave at St Gabriel's in 1996 she said:

[...] when Barbara came to Pimlico she was already well into churchgoing [...], and in London there were plenty of churches to choose from, but her experience had led her, [...] into wanting something higher, with more ritual, than the ones she was used to – and here was St Gabriel's right on her doorstep. (I think it might have been at this point that she bought [...] a little book called *The Ritual Reason Why* – not only, I might say, for her own enlightenment – and some amusement because it's written in question-and-answer form – but if she was also going to write about this kind of churchmanship, she must get it right.

In Robert Smith Pym found a lifelong friend. They had much in common, the church, books, and the same sort of humour. Together they went on 'church crawls'.

Anglo-Catholic churches and ritual and all that it implied in Hazel Holt's words in *A Lot to Ask* –

the fascinating names of the various kinds of incense, the celibate clergy with their cloaks and birettas, the days of obligation, 'all those Sundays after Trinity' – provided richness indeed to someone with an observant and ironic eye. (151)

The names of the various kinds of incense are fascinating indeed. For Rocky Napier in *EW* the promise of incense is an inducement to attend a service.

'High Mass – with music and incense? Oh, I should like that,' he said. 'I hope it is the best quality incense? I believe it varies.'
    'Yes, I've seen advertisements,' I admitted, 'and they have different names. Lambeth is very expensive, but Pax is quite cheap. It seems as if it ought to be the other way round.' (*EW*, 33)

Edwin and Father G. in *QIA*, talking church-shop, discuss 'whether to order a stronger brand of incense now that the Rosa Mystica was nearly finished' (*QIA*, 15).

Incense appears time and again in Pym's novels, and not only in churches, and becomes a sort of leitmotif.

Wilmet and Piers, walking by the river, pass a furniture depository, and joke about furniture being riddled with woodworm.

'It might be fitting to hold a kind of religious service over furniture as it enters the depository. Undenominational, do you think, like the chapel of a crematorium?'

'Oh, no,' I protested, 'surely there would be incense. Think how hygienic it would be – the very strongest kind of incense to smoke out the woodworm!' (*AGOB*, 71)

Even in a pub there may be a smell of incense. Mildred takes a sip of beer and looks round the room.

Being so near St Ermin's gave it an almost ecclesiastical air, especially as there was much mahagony, and I was fanciful enough to imagine that I even detected a faint smell of incense. (*EW*, 132)

The smell of incense has always been considered by Protestants to be the most aggressively Romish liturgical practice. This is reflected in scenes from *JP* and *EW*.

Incense is out of discussion in Nicholas Cleveland's parish church in *JP*. Jane only half-jokingly fantasizes after Canon and Mrs Pritchard's visit to the vicarage,

I suppose he just came to have a look at things. Perhaps they would peep into the church [...] to see if they could detect any smell of incense or other Popish innovations. (*JP*, 151)

Mildred, a clergyman's daughter, frequents St Mary's, an Anglo-Catholic church. For her family that would have been out of the question.

There were two churches in our district, but I had chosen St Mary's rather than All Souls', not only because it was nearer, but because it was 'High'. I am afraid my poor father and mother would not have approved at all and I could imagine my mother, her lips pursed, shaking her head and breathing in a frightened whisper, *'Incense'*. But perhaps it was only natural that I should want to rebel against my upbringing, even if only in such a harmless way. (*EW*, 12)

When incense is used liturgically, it is placed in a thurible or censer and swung by a server called thurifer. Tom Dagnall in *AFGL* is glad that Dr G.'s Anglo-Catholic clergyman-brother will not come to caretake in the house,

for on one occasion he had been rather too eager to help out with church services and it had been embarrassing having to admit that they never had incense and possessed neither thurible nor thurifer. (*AFGL*, 112)

In *STG* Belinda checks her sister's praise of Father Plowman's sensible sermons with intimations of terror.

'But Harriet,' said Belinda anxiously, 'he is rather high. He wears a biretta and has incense in the church. It's all so – well – Romish.' Broad-minded a she was, Belinda was unable to keep a note of horror out of her voice. (*STG*, 21)

Belinda here mentions an unmistakable sign of an Anglo-Catholic clergyman, namely the biretta. What is the biretta? *The Ritual Reason Why* which Pym liked to consult in all questions of Anglo-Catholic etiquette defines the biretta as

a square cap of black silk or other stuff, worn by parsons in Holy Orders at processions and other outdoor functions. (48)

Incidentally, Anglo-Catholicism has been nicknamed the 'London, Brighton and South Coast religion', and the south-east corner of the country has been called England's 'biretta belt'.

Mildred thinks that birettas in the hall are eminently suitable for celibate Anglo-Catholic clergymen.

[...] perhaps it is more suitable that a High Church clergyman should remain unmarried, that there should be a biretta in the hall rather than a perambulator. (*EW*, 16)

Celibacy of the clergy has always been a tenet of Anglo-Catholicism. The norm that Anglo-Catholic clergy should not marry is expressed in the phrase 'committing matrimony', suggesting an act not far short of adultery. Something of this comes out in *AGOB*.

Ransome's engagement comes as a shock to Father Thames and his housekeeper Wilf Bason at the clergy house. 'Celibacy of the clergy has always been our motto' (*AGOB*, 233) says Mr Bason and Father Thames echoes, 'Oh, it is *too* bad, *too* bad' (*AGOB*, 235).

What else do Anglo-Catholic clergymen wear? Neville Forbes has gone in flight from a woman in his parish to the West Country where his mother keeps a hotel at the seaside. Mrs Forbes is not too pleased about her son wandering around in his cassock.

'Well, Mam,' said Neville appearing in the doorway. The childish abbreviation sounded strange coming from a cassocked priest. [...]
'What do you want to go about in that old black cassock for?' she asked rather irritably.
'It's the uniform of a priest you know,' he said seriously. 'You'd find many in London who went about in their cassocks.'
'Oh, London ...' She made a contemptuous gesture. 'You look like some old monk. Still, I suppose it saves your other clothes – like wearing an overall.' (*NFRL*, 177)

A cassock is a long tunic confined at the waist by a broad sash. It may be buttoned from neck to foot and is usually black.

The vestments of the priest celebrating Mass are called Eucharistic vestments. In the Church of England these vestments fell into complete disuse for two centuries after the Reformation. In the 19th century the Anglo-Catholics reintroduced them, which aroused much opposition. Pym mentions some of these vestments in her fiction.

When in *LTA* Father Tulliver's wife falls ill, Rhoda Wellcome, Deirdre's aunt, a paragon of an *excellent woman*, kindly agrees to wash his albs.

The alb is a long white linen tunic with tight sleeves, reaching to the feet. It is belted at the waist.

'I hadn't a clean alb left and I'm not much of a hand at laundering,' he laughed, with the confidence of one who has never tried and does not intend to. 'You have a good drying ground at the back of the house, I suppose?'

'Yes, I shall hang the albs in the yard,' Rhoda pronounced solemnly. 'Of course we don't hang washing in the garden itself, it wouldn't do here. People wouldn't like it, although our neighbour Mrs Lovell isn't always guiltless in that respect.'

'Oh, certainly, I understand that some garments might not look well in a garden, but something of an ecclesiastical nature, surely that might be condoned?'

'The Lovells are not churchpeople,' Rhoda declared. 'I doubt if they would realize that the washing was of an – er – ecclesiastical nature.' She had found the last two words rather difficult to pronounce and hoped that Father Tulliver hadn't noticed. (*LTA*, 140)

Some days later

Deirdre opened the kitchen door but could not at first see Rhoda because the whole room seemed to be filled with voluminous white garments hanging from the clothes-airer and dripping on to the floor. 'What on earth have you been doing?' she asked.

'Oh, it's Father Tulliver's albs,' said Rhoda fussily. 'I washed them after lunch and now it's come on to rain. I don't know *how* I am going to get them dry.' (*LTA*, 168)

The surplice is a white linen garment of variable length with full sleeves. The cotta is a short surplice.

The cope is a vestment in the form of a mantle reaching to the heels, open in front, fastened at the breast with a clasp. It is worn in processions and on solemn occasions.

On Whit Sunday, Jean-Pierre Rossignol, an anthropologist, comes to the service at the suburban church near Deirdre's home. The church is based on St Michael's, Barnes.

As it was a Festival the servers were in their lace trimmed cottas and Father Tulliver was wearing a particularly splendid cope. (*LTA*, 78)

The term 'Mass' for the Eucharist, the Sacrament of the Lord's Supper, is a hallmark of Anglo-Catholicism. When the Archdeacon gives out the notices of the Christmas services he takes

the opportunity to say a few words of warning to those who intended to go to Midnight Mass at Father Plowman's church, dwelling darkly on the dangers they might meet there and pronouncing the word Rome with such horrifying emphasis that many of his hearers were quite alarmed. (*STG*, 201)

Tom Dagnall, the middle-of-the-road rector, dare not call his midnight service 'Mass'.

In *NFRL* Dulcie reads from the weather-beaten brown notice-board of St Ivel's 'Solemn Evensong and Benediction':

'What a lot they're giving us!'

'Oh, it's the usual kind of service in Anglo-Catholic churches,' said Viola in a superior tone. (*NFRL*, 161)

In Solemn Benediction, a Roman-Catholic extra-liturgical service, a large host is exposed to view in a monstrance and censed. The congregation is blessed with the host. To Jane, Solemn Evensong is the epitome of wickedness because it is so very Romish. At the end of a day in London Jane longs to be very wicked indeed but it is time to go to the station for the train.

It would have been nice to have tea in the Corner House or gone, rather wickedly, to a Solemn Evensong with lots of incense, she thought. (*JP*, 76)

An element of naughtiness, a sense of tasting forbidden fruit is also to be found in the description of a Corpus Christi procession in *AGOB*.

The procession round the church with lighted candles reminded me of a scene from an Italian opera – *Tosca*, I suppose. There was something daring and Romish about the whole thing which added to one's enjoyment. It should have been followed, I felt, by a reception in some magnificent palazzo, where we would drink splendid Italian wines with names like Asti Spumante, Lachryma Christi and Soave di Verona. That it seemed to go equally well with the tea and sandwiches and cakes in the church hall was perhaps a tribute to the catholicity of the Church of England. (*AGOB*, 203)

Pym herself writes in her diary:

The church ought to have a lot of summer festivals – Corpus Christi or St Peter and St Paul would do – so that we can have an evening Mass with lots of incense, all doors open and hymns with soppy words and Romish tunes. (*AVPE*, 202f.)

The Anglo-Catholic tradition has put high emphasis on sacramental confession. In the 19th century private confession to a priest gave rise to great controversy. The rite was stigmatized as extremely papistical. This still reverberates in Pym's fiction.

Harry Talbot, the husband of Wilmet's friend Rowena, gets very angry when Wilmet asks him whether their new vicar hears confessions.

'I suppose he hears confessions?' I asked rather naughtily.

'Heavens, don't talk about *that*!' Harry was almost purple in the face. 'He preached a sermon about it. Disgraceful! Some people walked out.' (*AGOB*, 89)

Mrs Trapnell in Prudence's office lowers her voice when she mentions that in her church, which is much too high for her, the vicar hears confessions. Dulcie, stepping into the porch of St Ivel's, reads with a shudder on the notice-board 'Confessions – Saturday 6.45'.

In a letter to Robert Smith, a comment on All Saints', Margaret Street shows Pym's ironic spirit at its best:

I emerged exhausted from Marks and Spencers wondering where on earth I could go to sit down [...] and suddenly thought of All Saints Margaret Street, which turned out to be deliciously cool and restful and only one lady there – no violet-stoled priests lurking to force Anglican ladies to make their Confessions. (*AVPE*, 207)

It still comes as a surprise to many people to realise that there are religious orders within the Church of England. Sisterhoods and communities of men were founded in the wake of the Oxford Movement. They made many people uneasy and evoked the hostility of those who objected to anything Romish. One still catches this feeling in some of Pym's novels.

When in *AGOB* Mary Beamish announces her intention to test her vocation at St Hildelith's Wilmet is shocked and thinks of it as a kind of imprisonment. Later she goes to see Mary at the convent.

A nun with steel-rimmed spectacles, and the pale lips and eyes that I always find so sinister, opened the door and smiled at me in a guarded remote sort of way. I felt that she could see right into my mind and knew all that I had been thinking about Piers. (*AGOB*, 160)

She took me through a side door and along a narrow path shaded with lilac bushes. I continued to look around anxiously, though I told myself that it was absurd to have this suspicious Protestant attitude towards convents. (*AGOB*, 161)

When in *AUA* Ianthe collides with a nun on the escalator in an underground station, a fellow passenger comments on the scene.

I don't think they ought to let them out, walking about like that in those black clothes. It gives me the creeps and I know it frightened the kiddies. I mean it's *not very nice*, is it. (*AUA*, 136)

There is no church presence in *TSDD* but there is an allusion to Anglican nuns. Miss Foxe, Leonora Eyre's tenant, moves to St Basil's Priory.

'It's St Basil's Priory,' Miss Foxe went on, as if Leonora would know at once what she meant. 'A delightful country house for elderly people run by Anglican nuns,' she explained,' and they've agreed to take me in.'

She made herself sound like a fallen woman, Leonora thought, being 'taken in' by nuns. (*TSDD*, 100)

The use of incense, birettas and eucharistic vestments, celibacy of the clergy, Mass, Benediction, confession, religious orders – all these things arouse suspicion and uneasiness among the supporters of the lower stratum of Anglicanism.

'Romish' or 'Popish' are the keywords in this context. The allurements of the Roman Catholic Church feature in most of Pym's novels. A visit to a religious bookshop by Jane is turned into a parable on Low, High, and Roman Church.

'Can I help you, madam? I asked an assistant. [...]

'No; thank you. I was just looking round' was what one usually said. Just looking round the Anglican Church, from one extreme to the other, perhaps climbing higher and higher, peeping over the top to have a look at Rome on the other side, and then quickly drawing back. (*JP*, 218)

Jane draws back; but for others the allurements of Rome are too strong, they 'go over' or 'go to Auntie', 'cross over', 'swim the Tiber', 'submit' or 'pope', like Father Sainsbury in *AGOB* or Adam Prince in *AFGL*.

Father Ransome may be tempted to go over, but the scooter and Mary Beamish keep his mind firmly on the good Anglican path (*AGOB*, 225).

Father Mark Ainger is another Anglo-Catholic priest who has toyed with the idea of 'poping', but he

was too old now and the whole thing was altogether too complicated. There was Sophia too, his beloved wife, and even Faustina who was, he felt sure, fiercely Protestant. (*AUA*, 144)

Having read Evelyn Waugh's life of Ronald Knox Pym writes to Robert Smith:

[I] thought what a pity it was he ever went over to Rome and how beastly it must be for a priest to do it and become a Roman priest. (*AVPE*, 208)

There are also lay people in Pym's novels who are converts, such as the two governesses moving into the Napiers' flat. And there are 'poor' Mr and Mrs Lake and Miss Spicer in *EW*. When they are mentioned by some parishioners of St Mary's there follows a short silence –

as is sometimes customary after speaking of the dead, though in this case the people referred to might have been thought to have met with a fate worse than death, for they had left us and been received into the Church of Rome. (*EW*, 214)

Janice Rossen states that not since Anthony Trollope's Barchester novels has the Anglican Church received such minute and detailed treatment in fiction.

On the other hand, Pym's novels have been criticised for being nearly empty of openly recounted spiritual experience, but I would rather support Charles Burkhart's claim in *The Pleasure of Miss Pym* that her faith was important to her but tremendously private in terms of its articulation.

Many critics have also focussed on what they call her satiric attitude toward the Church, but I would say she deals with the Church of England and Anglo-Catholicism in an ironic, yet kindly light. Pym herself says about her critical but affectionate attitude toward the Church:

I suppose I criticise and mock at the clergy and the Church of England because I am fond of them. (*PYM MS* 98, fol. 85)

Pym uses the Church of England, particularly the Anglo-Catholic wing, as a social milieu, as rich material for all kinds of human oddity. In this respect she has much in common with John Betjeman's particular brand of 'churchiness'.

Pym remarked on more than one occasion:

The Anglican Church and English literature, these are the two important things in my life and I would hardly know which order to put them in.

Her love of English literature and her love of the Church find reflection in a quotation from *Ode to a Nightingale* in *EW*.

After Allegra Gray's departure Julian Malory comes to see Mildred.

'I know the kind of person I should like to marry,' he went on, 'and I thought I had found her. But perhaps I looked too far and there might have been somebody nearer at hand.' [...]

'I cannot see what flowers are at my feet,' said Julian softly.

Nor what soft incense hangs upon the boughs, I continued to myself, feeling that the quotation had gone wrong somewhere and that it was not really quite what Julian had intended.

'That's Keats, isn't it?' I asked rather bluntly. 'I always think Nor What Soft Incense would be a splendid title for a novel. Perhaps about a village where there were two rival churches, one High and one Low. I wonder if it has ever been used?' (EW, 196)

One wishes that Pym might have written it.

Works cited

AFGLA A Few Green Leaves 1980. London: Flamingo, 1994

AGOB A Glass of Blessings. 1958. London: Pan Books in association with Jonathan Cape, 1994.

AUAA An Unsuitable Attachment. Ed. Hazel Holt. London, 1993

AVPE A Very Private Eye: The Diaries, Letters and Notebooks of Barbara Pym. 1984. Ed. Hazel Holt and Hilary Pym. London: Macmillan, 1984

EW Excellent Women. 1952. London: Pan Books, 1995

LTA Less Than Angels. 1955. London: Pan Books, 1993

NFR No Fond Return of Love. 1961. London: Pan Books in association with Jonathan Cape, 1993.

QIA Quartet in Autumn. 1977. London: Flamingo, 1994

STG Some Tame Gazelle. 1950. London: Pan Books, 1991

TSDD The Sweet Dove Died. 1978. London: Flamingo, 1994

PYM MS The papers of Barbara Pym. Department of Western Manuscripts, Bodleian Library, Oxford. Cited in the text by manuscript and folio number.

Selected secondary sources

Burkhart, Charles. *The Pleasure of Miss Pym*. Austin: Univ.Texas Press, 1987

Pym, Hilary Walton. "Barbara Pym in Pimlico". Unpublished manuscript of a talk given at St Gabriel's, Warwick Square, London, 14th February 1996

Rossen, Janice. *The World of Barbara Pym*. London: Macmillan, 1987

Shell, Alison. Barbara Pym and Ordinary Oxford. *Green Leaves*, 6(1), May 2000, pp.10-11.

Walker, Charles. *The Ritual Reason Why*. 2nd ed, London: J.T.Hayes, 1866

Birds, woodworm and Jesuits:
Roman Catholicism in Pym's novels

Joy Grant

Had the church been older and darker and smaller, had it perhaps been a Roman
Catholic church, I thought wickedly.

Mildred Lathbury in *Excellent Women* has slipped into her Anglican parish church
to meditate a while, only to find it sadly lacking in atmosphere. Would she have
drawn more comfort from a Roman Catholic church, she asks herself – but only
for a split second, for Mildred (most conscientious of Pym heroines) knows a
naughty thought when she has one, and considering how much it would have upset
her mother, that was a naughty thought indeed.

The late Mrs Lathbury, wife of a Low Church parson, was given to pursing her
lips and "breathing in a frightened whisper, 'Incense'", even in Anglo-Catholic
surroundings: it was the suggestion of Rome that upset her, as it did others in
Mildred's life. Her friend Dora grasps her umbrella and waves it like a sword at
the thought of entering the monks' enclosure at Buckfast Abbey, her cleaning lady
is shattered by relatives' comments on her style of worship: "They said it was
Roman Catholic or something and we'd all be kissing the Pope's toe before you
could say knife", while her dinner hostess, Mrs Bone, issues the strongest
warnings against birds, woodworm and the Society of Jesus:

"The Jesuits got my son, you know. You would hardly believe the things that
go on in their seminaries. I can lend you some very informative pamphlets."

– no doubt from the Protestant Trust Society, whose bookshop was near Barbara's
place of work.

Barbara distanced herself from rank prejudice of this kind by laughing at it. A
more reasoned approach was looked for in the Anglo-Catholic circles in which
she moved, where a priest might use a sermon to "explain about the Pope", like
Julian Mallory, or to tell "Why I am not a Roman Catholic", like Mark Ainger.
In point of fact, so close were the two churches in doctrine and ceremonial that it
was only right to remind people of the real differences, lest some of them be
tempted to jump the gap. As the main reasons for departures from her North
London congregation, Barbara listed "Rome, Death and Umbrage" (and the
greatest of these was Umbrage!).

Any emotional crisis – a broken engagement, for example – could in theory
send a priest over the edge, make him leave this Church of England, convert to
Rome and end up a cardinal, as was feared for Father Mallory in *Excellent Women*.
We know how Barbara regarded such behaviour from her comment on that bright
young Anglican hopeful, Ronald Knox: "I thought what a pity it was he ever went
over to Rome and how beastly it must be for a priest to do it and become a Roman
priest". Strong words!

Father Sainsbury in *A Glass of Blessings* becomes "Poor Edwin" from the moment he takes the plunge at Westminster Cathedral, "which seems a little less sinister than Farm Street, don't you think?" remarks Father Ransome (many a notable fish was caught in Peter's net by divine grace and the Jesuits of Mayfair). "Couldn't the Romans have welcomed him with a party?" asks Wilmet Forsyth, determined to be aggrieved for the victim's sake, and Ransome replies: "They've been coming so thick and fast lately – the converts, I mean, I suppose they couldn't welcome each one individually". Father Sainsbury had joined the exodus of 1955, in protest against the Anglican attitude to the Church of South India, some of whose clergy were not episcopally ordained. Father Thames, it may be recalled, thought of arranging some discussion groups on the issue, but dropped the idea. It was too hot a potato.

While over the years a great many Anglo-Catholic priests came under Barbara's eye, her contact with the Roman clergy was restricted to various priest-anthropologists met in the course of her work at *Africa*: Father Van Buick (notable for having taken a plastic portable altar into the field) was the model for Father Gemini in *Less Than Angels*, the Italian missionary who memorably throws off his clothes, and is suspected of securing a research grant by devious means ("I can't help feeling that the Jesuits are behind this", says Miss Clovis). Her Roman Catholic parish priests make only fleeting appearances: no sooner do we catch the lilt of their – invariably – Irish voices than they're gone. An endearing "Bye-bye now!" is all we have of Father Bogart in *Excellent Women,* while the well-meant platitudes of the young hospital chaplain in *Quartet in Autumn* abruptly cease when Marcia tells him she is not a Catholic: 'Ah then, you'll be a Protestant'. The violence of the word has a stunning effect, as it must to anyone used to the vaguer and gentler 'Anglican' or 'Church of England'. 'Well, it's nice to have had this chat. The Protestant chaplain will be along to see you." An altogether foreign encounter, not really typical of the mid 1970s when the Irish church was despatching fewer priests on what was jokingly termed the English mission.

Far from being sinister (though clad in strictest black), Barbara's priests are full of manly good cheer:

> "And you'll have the *Limerick Times* with the account of the hurling?" cries one Father to another at the airport. "A grand match it was, a grand match." "Did ye get the little bottles?" demands a jolly-looking curly-haired Irishman with a strong brogue of a fellow reverend newly landed in the Eternal City.

Anything more remote from the world of Father Thames and his Fabergé eggs is hard to imagine.

When it comes to the R.C. laity, Barbara is selective, ignoring both the"Old Catholic Families who kept the Faith alive in Penal Times" (and were so much admired by Evelyn Waugh) and the average English Catholic. Barbara's cradle Catholic is either Irish or quaintly Continental, like the Gallic anthropologist Jean-Pierre le Rossignol in *Less than Angels*, who bafflingly describes himself as a Thomist, and spends his Sundays sampling the various brands and flavours of English Protestantism.

She gives us a handful of English converts, a blunt term out of favour nowadays. Richly comic is Mildred Lathbury's introduction to a pair of cultured English spinsters:

> I gathered that they had 'gone over' in Italy, which seemed a suitable place to do it in, if one bad to do it at all. 'There was really no English church where we were,' said Miss Boniface almost apologetically, 'We didn't care for the priest either, he was very Low'. 'And the congregation was rather snobbish and unfriendly,' said Miss Edgar.
> 'You see, Bony and I were governesses and they were mostly titled people.'

The friends are well aware that their curious conduct will be more readily understood and forgiven if explained, not in theological terms, but in terms of social class, that most English of preoccupations. Had they too been coached by Jesuits?

One must remind oneself how very set in her ways, how proudly separate from other Christian bodies, was the English Catholic church that confronted Barbara and her fictional converts in the 1950s. The Latin Mass was offered by the priest with his back to the congregation, and in a lowered voice, as from time immemorial. Nuns still wore their antique habits. A priest's celibacy was seen as his crowning glory, and the idea of women Roman Catholic priests had not been mooted. The well-disciplined faithful – forbidden to worship in non-Catholic churches - were late in the decade actually granted permission to say the Lord's Prayer with other Christians in certain circumstances.

The sweeping changes initiated by the Second Vatican Council (1962-65), both in the liturgy and in inter-Church relationships, as reflected in *A Few Green Leaves*, date from the late 1970s – significantly, the only Pym novel in which a Roman Catholic character has a sizeable role to play. Adam Prince, Anglo-Catholic clergyman turned Roman Catholic layman, is on easy terms with the Anglicans, dropping off a bundle of jumble at the vicarage for the parish sale without a second thought, and even advising the vicar on the selection of communion wines: a delicate point, since Adam left the Church of England because he doubted the validity of Anglican orders. These are hardly heroic stands for togetherness, but they mark an advance on a quarter-century earlier. To feel the difference, one has only to recall the indignation of Anglican Sister Blatt in *Excellent Women* (1951) when invited by a member of Father Bogart's congregation to look in on their jumble sale!

> 'Well, really, that woman has a nerve, inviting me over to *their* jumble sale next week and telling me that their new priest is a lovely man!'(EW Chapter 7)

Doing her bit for ecumenism, Barbara attended a new-style Roman Mass in her church at Finstock, and was not impressed: "very unthrilling, no incense ... very unbeautiful language. Methodist harvest festival was better!"; she could understand why there was a Latin Mass Society, she said. The vicar in the novel would agree. He feels sorry for Adam: "That dreadful vernacular Mass," he thinks, "scant consolation for one brought up on the 19th century Anglo-Catholic revival and *The Ritual Reason Why*".

But Adam makes no complaint, and whether driving off to Sunday Mass in his ruby-red Renault, or preparing a "rather special" dinner for Father Byrne (yet another priest with an Abbey Theatre accent) seems perfectly comfortable in the church of Rome.

Barbara herself felt no temptation to "go over". Happy with the Church of England, and having definite misgivings about Rome, her attitude was much like that of Jane Cleveland, the vicar's wife in *Jane and Prudence:* while wandering round the various departments of a large religious bookshop, Jane feels as though she were looking round the entire Anglican Church, from one extreme to the other:

> Climbing higher and higher, peeping over the top to have a look at Rome on the other side, and then quickly drawing back.

Communal rites: tea, wine and Milton in Barbara Pym's Novels

Judy B. McInnis

The mingling of sacred and profane love fascinated Barbara Pym as much as it did Milton, to whom she often alludes. Lotus Snow regards Milton as less important to Pym than were John Donne and George Herbert, primarily because of the indirect nature of Pym's Miltonic allusions. Analyzing the latter, I shall argue that Pym used Milton as a negative touchstone to define her feminist theology. Recently Wittreich (xi) and Gallagher (171) have defended Milton as an outstanding feminist of his time. On the other hand, Corum follows Gilbert and Gubar (180) by stressing Milton's patriarchal orthodoxy which he perceives as atonement for the poet's sinful rebelliousness. The perception of Milton as misogynist was the prevailing view in Pym's lifetime.

Milton endeavoured to distinguish sacred from profane love even in Eden. Raphael warns Adam:

> Love refines
> The thoughts, and heart enlarges, hath his seat
> In Reason and is judicious, is the scale
> By which to heavn'ly Love thou may'st ascend,
> Not sunk in carnal pleasure, for which cause
> Among the beasts no Mate for thee was found. *(Paradise Lost,* VIII:589-594)

The consequence of the fall in Milton, and in the Hebraic/Christian tradition he represents, is that Adam and Eve descend to bestial passion. Woman, associated with the body, draws man into the lower realm. As Eve tempts Adam and is the immediate cause of his fall, so Delilah tempts Samson and causes him to lose his physical prowess. In Milton's theology, God the Father is superior to Christ the Mediator, who is in turn superior to the Holy Spirit. Man is superior to woman as the spirit is to the flesh.

Pym establishes an inverse ordering of the trinity and everywhere questions man's superiority to woman. She establishes serving the body, woman's traditional role, as a means of fostering the spirit. I shall demonstrate Pym's subversive use of Milton through an investigation of the nature of love in relation to the rituals of tea and wine consumption in her novels. I believe Pym uses these rituals – feminine and masculine – to figure Caritas and Eros, the immanent and the transcendent, the real and the ideal. Ministering to the body, the rituals establish communal links between participants and, by providing solace for both body and spirit, imitate the transubstantiation of the Christian Mass.

Rubenstein has written of Pym's 'mingling the spiritual and mundane' (1987) to suggest 'that not only love but even the holy spirit calls us to and through the things of this world' (181). Yet Rubenstein juxtaposes 'tea and biscuits' with 'real spiritual sustenance' (173). Weld, on the contrary, argues that 'food for Pym has always been a social cohesive, joining partakers in pleasurable community and providing spiritual as well as physical comfort' (189). Aligning myself with Weld, I would further argue that 'tea and biscuits' provide the means to a development of Christian community. The continuity of the Church depends upon the survival of the body to which women minister.

With her Bakhtinian emphasis on the body, Pym fashioned her novels in the border region between satire and comedy. As Frye observes, old comedy ended with actors throwing 'bits of food to the audience' (192) who literally shared an act of communion to celebrate the renewal of society. In Pym's novels, this communion is reflected in the characters' sharing of tea and wine, whether in the formality of the 1930s or the casualness of the 70s. Rossen has pointed out that Pym never made her theology explicit (81). I believe that the outline of Pym's theology emerges from the conjunction of descriptions of tea, wine and Milton.

I should like to begin by way of a biographical episode establishing Pym's connection to Milton. Only those privy to this episode can fully appreciate both the significance and the humor of her glancing references to the English poet.

Pym, like her predecessors in the sacred parody tradition which evolved from the *Song of Songs*, through the medieval troubadours, through Petrarch's anguished sonnets to Laura, to the English poetic tradition of Wyatt, Surrey, Sidney, *et al.*, openly delighted in the titillating conjunction of the reverenced and the reviled'. Her affair with Henry Harvey culminated in a reading of *Samson Agonistes* in the nude – a reading interrupted when Henry's room-mate Robert Liddell (Jock) burst in upon the young lovers. From Pym's account of the episode it is apparent that she enjoyed this flagrant undercutting of the great English Puritan, an enjoyment increased by being discovered in so compromising a situation.[2]

In *Some Tame Gazelle* Pym at the age of twenty-one transformed life into art by projecting herself and her Oxford circle into the aged residents of an English village. In the novel Archdeacon Henry Hoccleve nostalgically reads *Samson Agonistes* to the timid, repressed spinster Belinda Bede. This poignant evening repeats their youth when Hoccleve courted Belinda by reading Milton – certainly not in the situation in which Henry Harvey actually read to Barbara Pym. It is all the recompense Belinda needs for her lifelong devotion to a man who not only chose to marry someone else but who daily reveals to Belinda and his other parishioners a vain, pompous, and lazy character. This recasting of the *Samson Agonistes* episode, chaste though it is, retains the conjunction of the sacred (love of the Deity, reason, and beauty) and the profane (the attraction Belinda and Henry feel for each other). The setting of the reading undermines Milton's patriarchal theology by suggesting that the lovers look for erotic rather than moral messages in the text. Milton is a poet Belinda wishes to share only with Hoccleve; she is horrified when Bishop Grote couches his patronizing and patriarchal marriage proposal in terms of *Paradise Lost*

From her home in Oswestry, Pym sent copies of her work, begun in July 1934, to Harvey and Robert Liddell. The latter replied in December 1934, with a poem in which he too recalls the *Samson Agonistes* episode, but makes Milton himself the seducer of Cassandra:

> Beholding her, the godlike Puritan
> Forgot his godhead, and became a man
> And prayed her as a second Eve to come
> And share his Eden in Elysium.
> Where he, John Milton, she, Cassandra Pym,
> (He for God only, she for God in him),
> Might live again the early days of Earth -
> Unwieldy elephants should give them Mirth,
> Only no serpent should be lurking there. ...
> And wish her CALM OF MIND, ALL PASSION SPENT. (13-14)

Liddell has adapted most of these lines from Book IV of *Paradise Lost*: 'he for God only, she for God in Him' (verse 299);

> ...th'unwieldy Elephant
> To make them mirth us'd all his might, and wreath'd
> His lithe Proboscis; close the Serpent sly' (verses 345-347).

His last line echoes the last line of *Samson Agonistes* when Pym escapes to her ivory Tower ,'all passion spent.' He depicts her in retirement where she devotes herself to domestic tasks and reads only the chastest poets. In fact, Liddell's poem accompanied a copy of the verses, not of John Milton, but of the notorious John Wilmot, Earl of Rochester, the Restoration rake who slyly declared his scabrous poetry fit for the chaste ears of matrons. Both in this gesture and within his witty verses Liddell underscored Pym's standing of John Milton on his head.

Pym continued to allude playfully to Milton in her other novels, but never so insistently as in *Some Tame Gazelle* and *Crampton Hodnet*, her first two novels written under Harvey's spell. The allusion may be as tangential as the name Allegra Grey in *Excellent Women*: Allegra's name recalls the promise of happy married life in Milton's 'L'Allegro.' In *An Unsuitable Attachment* (252) Basil Branche foresees the happiness of Ianthe Broom and John Challow:

> 'Imparadised in one another's arms, as Milton put it,' Basil went on. 'Or encasseroled, perhaps – the bay leaf resting on the boeufbourgignon.

In addition Snow notes that Jane (in *Jane and Prudence*) quotes from *Samson Agonistes* as does Leonora Eyre (TSDD) and 'that Comus is alluded to in *Some Tame Gazelle* and *Less Than Angels*; the sonnet 'When I consider how my light is spent' in *Excellent Women* and Milton's metrical version of Psalm 136, 'Let us with gladsome mind' in JAP (124). Ironic as these allusions may be in light of the *Samson Agonistes* episode, they still evoke Milton's patriarchal theology and invite the readers to compare his views with those of Pym's mid-twentieth-century characters.

Pym's evocation of the 'impure' blending of profane and sacred love serves as the background against which she contrasts her characters' ideal visions of themselves and others with the reality of their lives. In her novels the chasm between the real and the ideal is bridged by the transforming power of desire and imagination. Through the impetus of Eros (passion) the lover seeks to unite with the perceived perfection of the Beloved. Once the lover discovers the Beloved's flaws, Caritas (charity) enables him or her to continue nurturing the bonds of affection. Defects become endearing quirks which, by revealing the human weakness of their possessor, elicit the lover's desire to protect the beloved. From its initiation in Eros, love within marriage pales into a habit of charitable forbearance. This scenario is played out in all of Pym's novels during ceremonies of the imbibing of tea and, sometimes, wine.

Not crises in the romantic lives of the characters, nor the exigencies of work, nor the obligations of religious devotion, disrupt the sanctity of the tea ritual. Indeed, catastrophe can sometimes be averted by the simple expedient of offering the victim a cup of tea. In Pym's early novel, *Excellent Women*, Mildred offers tea first to Rocky Napier then to Julian Malory, when they are overpowered by their problems with women; in the last novel, *A Few Green Leaves*, Emma likewise prepares tea and boiled eggs for Graham who has recently separated from his wife. Whenever a character feels unable to cope, a cup of tea restores his or her spirits and places things in proper perspective.

The ubiquity of the English tea in Pym's novels prevents cataloging all its instances, but a just idea of her uses of the ritual can be gained through examination of Crampton Hodnet. There its customary observance reassures Jessie Morrow that the Clevelands' marriage could not truly be endangered. That it is stems from Margaret Cleveland's failure to attend properly to her husband's tea and to her suggestion that he take one of his young students out for tea. Francis acts upon the suggestion and finds himself quoting poetry and falling in love with Barbara Bird over the teacups in Fuller's, as he had once courted his wife with renditions of 'To His Coy Mistress' over a cup of tea..

Meanwhile, Francis' daughter Anthea is locked in an embrace with Simon Beddoes in the latter's Oxford rooms, the tea which provided the ostensible occasion for the visit languishing on the fire. In the streets below a Salvation Army Band provides a comfortable background of hymns and later 'came the sound of the various bells calling people to evensong' (CH 38). Here Pym makes sacred love the soothing background for the profane love of two young people, who seek ecstasy if not salvation in each other. Instead of describing the lovemaking, Pym slyly suggests sexual excitation through the allusion to the rousing Salvation Army hymns, quiescence in the allusion to evensong bells.

Francis explains his absence to his wife with the elaborate fiction that he has been discussing *Paradise Lost* with Edwin Killigrew over tea. In another oblique allusion to Pym's *Samson Agonistes* episode with Henry Harvey, Francis declares his love to Barbara Bird as they gaze at Milton's signature in a Commonplace Book in the British Museum. Barbara returns to reality as she takes tea at Lyons': 'Milton couldn't really have written in the book they had been looking at, just as Francis couldn't really have said those words and she have agreed with them' (CH

100). Jessie Morrow muses over the gossip that Barbara and Francis have been seen in Lyons', and remembers a large Baroque white and gold temple: 'almost more suitable for sacred love than profane' (CH 124). Both the drama of Francis' return home after his aborted elopement to Paris with Miss Bird and the contiguous drama of his daughter's receipt of a 'Dear John' letter from Simon are assimilated and reduced to manageable proportion by their occurrence at teatime, the inexorable ritual they gratefully observe.

The minor characters of *Crampton Hodnet* are equally devoted to the tea ritual. Margaret Cleveland and Maude Doggett provide substantial teas for young Oxford students, occasions which allow them to make new friendships and to receive the unsolicited advice of the mother surrogate. Mrs Killigrew invites her friends to tea to impart gossip about Francis' infidelity and to force him back into the mould of a socially-acceptable role: either a divorced man or a faithful husband. Enlarging their social concern, church members hold charity teas, preferably presided over by some titled personage like Lady Beddoes (Bed-does), to benefit the poor or the foreign pagan.

In her other novels no less than in *Crampton Hodnet*, Pym develops the tea as a symbol of societal order and stability. A maternal ritual, usually presided over by women, the English tea provides both physical and spiritual communion. The ceremony nurtures the emotional bonds that tie society's members altogether in the relationships of lovers, family members, friends, workers, and religious observants. Mildred immediately repents her suggestion to forgo tea at a church committee meeting: 'my question had struck at something deep and fundamental. It was the kind of question that starts a landslide in the mind' (EW 227). The role of tea-pourer is jealously sought, for it corresponds to the sacramental role of high priest within the domestic sphere. Thus Fabian Driver (JAP) chooses to pour out tea himself rather than alienate either Jessie Morrow or Prudence by revealing his preference for one of them; Jessie subsequently expresses her resentment by spilling tea over Prudence's elegant gown. She completes her revenge later when she and Miss Doggett lead Fabian captive – 'like Samson' (JAP 215) - to their home. The vain, self-indulgent and philandering Fabian shares only a luxuriant head of hair with Samson and only his patriarchal sympathies with Milton. To relate Jesse to Delilah is to perceive that Pym counters Milton's treacherous spouse with a helpmeet morally superior to her husband.

In *An Unsuitable Attachment* Pym presents tea in an ecclesiastical setting. Rupert Stonebird recalls his mother's assumption of the sacramental role of tea-pourer, as she acted the counterpart of her husband the vicar who presided over the ritual of communion: 'He had not been to any of the social functions advertised – it would have seemed like living his life backwards to enter voluntarily a church hall full of women and cups of tea – he could see his mother at the urn and himself as a boy handing round those very cups' (AUA 35). In *A Glass of Blessings,* Pym underscores the sacramental nature of the tea ritual which is observed as part of the welcoming ceremonies for Father Ransome:

'I can see Mrs. Greenhill at the urn. Now we can get on to the main object of this gathering, eh, Ransome?' ... Father Bode stood rubbing his hands as she approached, attended by a kind of acolyte bearing cups of tea on a tray (60).

Near the end of the novel Pym has Ransome articulate the association of the English tea with society's continuity. 'Yes, life has to go on, and I suppose a cup of tea does make it seem to be doing that more than anything' (AGOB 210). Throughout Pym's novels tea restaurants are run by widows, often clergymen's widows, who function as modern versions of the ancient celibate female religious orders dedicated to the care of the temple.

The tea ceremony is no less integral to the work world than it is to family and church life. In *Jane and Prudence* and *Quartet in Autumn* the workers eagerly await their tea and are distressed by any variation in its observance. The unfortunate Esther Clovis in *Less than Angels* was reputed to have lost her job as secretary of a learned society because of the deficiencies in her tea-making. In *No Fond Return of Love,* the beverage and the smorgasbord method of presenting it at a charity function become symbolic of life itself. Aylwyn Forbes' tea 'tasted strong and bitter. Like Life? He wondered' (NFROL 15). When Dulcie is instructed that she must make a selection and then pay for what is on her plate, she observes that the procedure is 'rather like life ... Except that there you can't always choose exactly what you want' (NFROL 75).

While the tea ritual celebrates reality and the continuity of daily life assured by an immanent deity, the consumption of wine in the Eucharist represents the human attempt to achieve union with an ideal, transcendent divinity. A patriarchal ritual administered exclusively by male priests in Pym's novels, the Eucharist celebrates the extraordinary intervention of the divine in human affairs. The Anglican Church has avoided formally defining the sacrament. The Book of Common Prayer permits a wide range of interpretation from the belief in transubstantiation, upheld by the Roman Catholic Church and encouraged by the Oxford Movement, to the Calvinist doctrine of the spiritual, but not the material, transformation of the bread and wine. Most of Pym's protagonists are High Church – Latimer, Mildred, Wilmet, Ransome, Viola Dace, Fabian Driver, Everard Bone, Edwin Braithwaite – but they resist actual conversion to Rome. The reason may be aesthetic, sociological or theological. Mildred and Fabian Driver express distaste for disappointing English examples of Catholic architecture. Although Roman Catholicism represents an exotic, sensuous faith abroad, in England it has 'lower-class' Irish connections. Ransome remains steadfast in the Anglican Church because he is appalled at the lower-class tea provided in the Roman Catholic Church he visits. Pym's repressed Anglicans cannot escape Milton's rationalization *Of Church Dogma* nor their eighteenth-century Latitudinarian heritage. Mildred regrets the lack of opportunity for sentimental conversion to Rome in the hygienic abbey she visits: 'for there was no warm rosy darkness to hide in, no comfortable confusion of doctrines and dogmas; all would be reasoned out and clearly explained, as indeed it should be' (EW Chapter 21).

Still, Pym's characters frequently yearn for Roman sacramentalism or for evangelical Protestantism, both associated with the masses who express religion in image and gesture with greater physical freedom than Pym's middle-class characters. Letty Crowe remains outside the noisily joyous religious celebrations of her African landlord: her faith was 'a grey, formal, respectable thing of measured observances and mild general undemanding kindness to all' (QIA 66). Ianthe Broom (AUA) thinks "coloured people ... are more naturally religious than we are. It is the white people who are the heathen." Pym's interpreters have emphasized the formalistic character of worship in her novels (Burkhart 108) and its 'devitalisation' (Benet 513). Rossen lists numerous dangers to the Anglican Church: 'paganism, atheism, aestheticism, 'Rome,' English literature, attrition and a corresponding reverence for the medical profession' (95). Throughout her novels Pym suggests that the inhibited English should allow greater physical expression of their faith. Resplendent Rome offers greater hope of a spiritual renascence than Milton's grey Puritanism. Love in all its manifestations escapes Reason's careful gradations.

In *An Unsuitable Attachment,* Pym contrasts Italian culture dominated by wine and Eros with English culture dominated by tea and Caritas. To Ianthe, the force of desire is both more intense and more earthy among the Italians; in Italy young lovers 'gaze at each other more devouringly' and the Italian priest looks dirtier than his English counterpart (AUA 185). The Catholic priests on the plane to Italy prove to be a rowdy bunch who eagerly buy up the small bottles of alcohol. Much as Penelope Grandison desires to kiss St Peter's toe for good luck, 'when the moment came she couldn't do it. She became fiercely hygienic and Protestant and held back' (AUA 158). At the same time an Italian presses himself against her – 'within the very walls of the Church !' she indignantly fumes. Yet in Italy, where the party stays at the Pensione Laura, evocative of Petrarch's impassioned sonnets of unrequited love, both Ianthe and Penelope recognize their love for John and Rupert. The young women find a personal spiritual message in the neon sign 'Banco Di Santo Spirito' that glares out over the Roman landscape, as Londoners are strengthened by the sign 'Take Courage', even though 'Courage' is a beer and the bank is a commercial monetary establishment. The reader is reminded of the fairy tale association of golden coins with fertility. As Rubenstein points out, 'the Banco di Santo Spirito is an illuminated and illuminating repository of spirituality that resists definition' (181).

Sophia, the vicar's wife who organized the trip to Italy, muses on Anglo- and Roman Catholicism and wonders 'if the latter had need of nourishment from the former' (AUA 142). Actually the reverse is true, for Pym suggests throughout the novel that the Anglicans could use an injection of the more virile, earthy Roman faith. Imagination and desire are stronger in the Italians, who move so easily from the profane to the sacred, from Laura and Beatrice to the Virgin Mary. In their careful rationalizations the English do not so easily effect the transformations of love.

Pym symbolically demonstrates the invigoration which the visit to Rome effects upon her characters in the episode in which the quintessentially Protestant Sister Dew breaks her leg and is carried by two strong Italian men to the hospital. The incident proves to be not a disaster but the highpoint of Sister Dew's trip.

Since in Christian symbolism Dew signifies grace, Pym here indicates the condition and the cure for the hobbled Anglican faith.

Pym associates Roman artistic achievement with the more primitive, 'earthy', and 'virile' culture's ability to draw upon the reserves of the irrational and the subconscious. Vicar Mark Ainger, overwhelmed by the grandeur of St Peter's, realizes that the Anglicans have produced no comparable artistic marvel. He cannot conjure up an image of Canterbury cathedral, the nearest equivalent, but instead recalls a vignette 'of a tall thin English lady he and Sophia had once seen arranging long-stalked thornless red roses on the high altar one Saturday morning' (AUA 157). English roses do not draw blood, Pym suggests in an oblique reference to Christ's blood, transubstantiated in Communion wine.

Earlier in the novel Pym underscored the feminine nature of the Anglican Church by having Rupert describe it as having 'fewer people and even more cups of tea' than in his youth, to which Penelope protests: 'There should be more people and lots of wine' (AUA 84). Penelope perceives clergymen 'as not quite manly' despite their priestly function of enforcing patriarchal beliefs. She suspects Rupert's virility because he is not only a vicar's son but looks like a vicar himself. Furthermore, his career in anthropology strikes her as perhaps effeminate. Rupert himself entertains doubts about his manly role. He worries that 'he was showing himself to be not quite a man' in allowing the two vicars, Basil Branche and Mark Ainger, to select the wine for the party at the Italian restaurant. As de Paolo has pointed out, 'the not unexpected association of men and wine or liquor is merely a reflection of larger issues of self-evaluation and power' (4).

The other novels also reveal an ideal pattern of female dominance in the tea ritual and male dominance in the wine ritual, whether on the secular or the religious level. Thus Tom Dagnell and Martin Shrubsole discuss wine knowledgeably and consume more of it over dinner than Avice and her mother: "An excellent thing in women, this abstemiousness in wine-drinking, though it hadn't been quite what Lear or Shakespeare meant when they coined the phrase," thinks Tom (AFGL 186). Wilmet (AGOB) observes that women are not supposed to admit to a liking for port, and Piers Longbridge's exotic appeal lies in his having been raised in Portugal where his father was engaged in the wine trade. But when he and Wilmet meet for their first tryst, he suggests that they stop for tea, an indication that Wilmet's romance will never materialize. Aylwyn Forbes, who lists his hobbies as wine and conversation, prefers women not to 'be too knowledgeable about wine' (NFRL 123). Professor Felix Mainwaring (LTA), representative of the elite values of old English society, is pleased that the young voluptuous Vanessa defers to his choice of sherry, while the spinster Esther Clovis significantly reveals her distaste for the beverage.

Women defer to men's connoisseurship of wine, yet the ladies as often as the gentlemen provide the wine at those social gatherings marked by a strong undercurrent of sexual interest. Ianthe (AUA) offers sherry to her potential suitors; Jessie Morrow and Stephen Latimer (CH) flirt over stolen sherry; Wilmet plies sherry upon Ransome (AGOB); Catherine (LTA) guards an expensive bottle of wine against the day Tom will complete his thesis; Meg (TSDD) keeps a bottle of

Yugoslav Riesling in the refrigerator to celebrate Colin's periodic returns to her after interludes with his male lovers. Catherine (LTA) – in the process of buying a bottle of cheap red wine at the Greek restaurant she and Tom frequent – discovers herself supplanted by Deirdre Swan. Subsequently she is drawn to Alaric by their mutual hobby of collecting wine lists.

Male characters also initiate their profane amorous relationships with wine. Thus Everard Bone (EW) invites Mildred to dinner, the wine bottle warming beside the fire; Aylwyn Forbes (NFRL) presses sherry upon Laurel; Rupert Stonebird (AUA) entertains both potential marital candidates at a dinner replete with wine, then makes an overture to Ianthe over a glass of sherry. Tom Mallow (LTA) offers Deirdre Swan a glass of 'cold, sour red wine' which, much to her chagrin, she finds almost undrinkable. Francis Cleveland (CH) affords the most amusing example of male initiation of the wine-drinking ritual. Bent upon beginning a physical relationship with Barbara Bird, he images himself parading through the Oxford streets with a wine bottle protruding from beneath his coat, in a scene reminiscent of Aristophanic comedy. He carries the bottle more circumspectly, and, significantly, he forgets the corkscrew so that the bottle, like Barbara, remains a virgin.

As reserved in their lovemaking as in their consumption of wine, Pym's characters seldom consummate a union; her novels are nearly devoid of erotic descriptions. In *The Sweet Dove Died*, her most sensuous novel, James and Phoebe's clumsy love-making is ironically surpassed by that of James and Ned. Leonora Eyre, troubled by distasteful memories of a few remorseful bedroom scenes, repels Humphrey's physical overtures. While Prudence Bates (JAP) has fond memories of her past lovers, she recalls nothing to distinguish between them. Only the very young – an Anthea Cleveland (CH) or a Deirdre Swan (LTA), a Laurel (NFRL) or a Vanessa (LTA) actually seem to enjoy love-making. While Pym observes the comic convention to the exent of showing the reconciliation of male and female protagonists, she seldom supplies an account of the marriage. Thus the union of Mildred and Everard (EW) and that of Jessie and Fabian (JAP) occur in the hiatus between novels rather than in the text.

Pym's reticence in the description of Eros extends to her treatment of the Eucharist, the central sacrament of the Christian faith. Despite the assiduous detailing of ceremonies celebrating high holy days – Christmas, Easter, Whit Sunday, etc. – and numerous accounts of sermons, Pym does not explicitly describe communion. In *A Glass of Blessings*, Wilmet rejoices in a Sung Eucharist that few attend. Her devotion survives even Mr Coleman's kindling the New Fire on Holy Saturday with his cigarette lighter. Plain Mary Beamish acts as Wilmet's foil. A Christ-like figure in her chaste, humble, and selfless devotion to others, Mary delights in the Corpus Christi festival. In choosing to marry Ransome rather than to become a nun, she ironically relinquishes Eros, whose ultimate end is mystical union with God, for Caritas, unselfish love of others. She sacrifices single-minded pursuit of her own spiritual perfection for support of her Church's imperfect male priest. She, more than her fiancé Marius Lovejoy Ransome, promises to breathe new life into the parish both spiritually and materially, her money enabling the couple to repair the fungus-caused dry rot of the church. In the description of the Corpus Christi procession in which Wilmet and Mary participate, Wilmet in another of Pym's exchanges of the sacred and the profane is reminded both of Tosca and of Roman Catholic services. She perceives tea and wine as equally sacramental rituals, though the former marks the British character:

> It should have been followed, I felt, by a reception in some magnificent palazzo, where we would drink splendid Italian wines with names like Asti Spumante, Lachryma Christi and Soave di Verona. That it seemed to go equally well with the tea and sandwiches and cakes in the church hall was perhaps a tribute to the true catholicity of the Church of England (AGOB 297).

Pym alludes obliquely to sacred love in *The Sweet Dove Died*, whose title recalls the Holy Ghost, spirit of love. The characters in the novel have substituted art for religion. Living only for self, they fail to establish meaningful love relationships on the profane level as well. Leonora Eyre, a fiftyish '*belle dame sans merci*', feels disgust for the sexual basis of religion. When she sees a working-class family clustered around a totem pole at Virginia Water, she comments to herself, 'What a hideous phallic symbol ... but of course one wouldn't mention it, only hurry by with head averted' (TSDD 37). Humbled by James' abandonment of her for Ned, she consoles herself with tea, 'a drink she did not much like because of the comfort it was said to bring to those whom she normally despised' (TSDD 161). She drinks it frequently thereafter as she learns to admit her need of comfort and sustenance from other human beings.

In *Quartet in Autumn* Pym describes a communion which demonstrates her typical exchange between profane and sacred love as well as the exchange between secular and sacred ceremonies. After Marcia Ivory dies, her friends discover that this woman, who never allowed alcohol to pass her lips, had hidden away a bottle of Queen of Sheba sherry. They open and drink it in remembrance of her. Through her physical and mental torment, Marcia becomes a macabre Christ figure whose death brings grace to those still living, cementing the tenuous bonds that hold them together and giving new purpose to Norman, the most socially unassimilated among them. In this novel, as in *The Sweet Dove Died*, Pym reveals the importance of the Holy Spirit in establishing communion between people. It is obvious that for her the Spirit was of greater importance than God the Father and Christ the Mediator; her hierarchy reverses Milton's.

A Few Green Leaves is a dense mosaic of themes treated in the earlier novels. The title refers to the aging female parishioners' insertion of new greenery around the fading roses on the Church's altar. Benet interprets this to mean that 'the revitalization of the Church (which is traditionally the Rose of Sharon) depends upon the infusion of a fresh faith in its beauty and capacity to serve' (512). Tom Dagnell, a vicar whose name summons up the sounding of evening bells, threatens to let his ministry sink into historical oblivion as he cultivates his interest in DMVs (deserted medieval villages). The woods of San Greal harbor a mean housing development and an abandoned, stinking poultry house, formerly managed by Jason Dyer. These names evoke the failure both of the myth of the Holy Grail and that of Jason and the Golden Fleece. The name of Martin Shrubsole indicates the spiritual suicide of the scientific elite who are appropriating the vicar's former authority. The agnostic doctor has the soul of one of Dante's speaking shrubs. Another male character, Adam Prince, has declined irreparably from his Biblical and Miltonic antecedents by abandoning his position as an Anglican vicar to become food critic for a journal. He seems to feel more the loss of the gustatory pleasure of consuming Communion wine than the gain of any spiritual good in his conversion to Roman Catholicism. When he donates a bottle of wine to the Anglican Church's 'bring and buy sale', its elderly female recipient exchanges it for a barbola mirror. Her action figures the narcissism and lack of vitality of the older women who make up most of the congregation. Pym signals the transfer of power to the emerging village elite when the bottle is carried off by the young energetic doctor's wife. The latter's fidelity to the church countermands to some degree her position as appendage to the scientific community.

Pym's reaffirmation of her theology of love is most clearly seen in three significant choices her heroine Emma makes. First, she decides to abandon her career as anthropologist, scientific observer of humanity, for that of novelist, humanistic observer. Second, she decides to concentrate her romantic aspirations on the vicar Dagnell rather than on the media personality Graham. Third, she remains faithful to the Church, the only institution to provide consolation in death. Emma is relieved that Tom dissuaded Miss Lickerish's surviving relatives from using a funeral hymn with a suggestion of wormlike submission to God, a quality so little displayed by the stalwart, independent woman. Emma perceives:

> The Almighty, a nebulous figure, and seated on his right her headmistress, eyes gleaming but kindly behind rimless glasses which in an earlier age would have been pince-nez (AFGL 88).

This image of a woman, rather like Miss Lickerish, suggests that God's real power, his right hand, his Miltonic propagandist, is a woman who conveniently creates the myth of male omnipotence to conceal her own manipulation of the shuttle in weaving life's tapestry. Women are responsible for defining the moral code which, internalised, becomes God. Emma's image recalls Mrs Lord (NFROL), a cleaning woman, and Mrs Pope (QIA), an aging landlady, both of whom represent the English moral code formalized in the Anglican church.

Near the end of *A Few Green Leaves*, Emma attends a midnight Christmas Eve service at which Geoffrey Poor, the non-believing organist, plays *The Messiah* magnificently, perhaps the effect of the apricot brandy Tom has given him. In this anomalous situation, Pym incarnates the relationship of Eros and Caritas: the believer Tom shows his love of his neighbor (Caritas) with the gift of brandy, which, with 'the opportunity of playing on a fine instrument' (AFGL 238), inspires 'poor' Geoffrey to the perfection of his art (Eros). The reader perceives the beauty the Church has contributed to society, a beauty that still draws a large congregation on high holy days.

At this service, in another example of Pym's exchange between sacred and profane love, Emma realizes that she wants a male companion. She has as much difficulty envisioning him as she did God:

> Some nebulous, comfortable – even handsome – figure suggested itself, which made her realize that even the most cynical and sophisticated woman is not, at times, altogether out of sympathy with the ideas of the romantic novelist (AFGL 239).

The reader recognizes that this figure is Tom Dagnell, who has awakened Emma's affection both by his beauty (Eros) and by his pathos (Caritas). For Emma profane and sacred love are mixed. Her perception of the Deity mirrors her perception of a husband. Furthermore, the feminine has become inextricably mixed with the perception of the male divinity and proves the more effectual in life's daily affairs.

Patriarchal religion and society are on the wane, but Pym's characters continue to cultivate the old ideal. 'Man and woman created he them',[3] Tom ruefully comments at the beginning of the novel when he catches sight of Robbie and Tamsin Barraclough, the former dictating to the latter who was seated at the typewriter. In her last novel, Pym returned to the Biblical scene recreated by John Milton dictating *Paradise Lost* to his daughters.

Throughout her novels Pym developed the rituals of tea and wine as metonymic of the feminine and the masculine, Caritas and Eros, the immanent and the transcendent. Caritas dominates but it must be awakened by Eros; the many cups of tea sometimes enlivened by a glass of wine. Strauss-Noll has pointed out that Pym's female characters sometimes balk at taking up the wife's role. Her male characters likewise experience difficulty supplying the erotic spark in a feminised society which has exposed the secrets of male privilege.

Nevertheless, Pym was not yet willing to pronounce the patriarchal God of the JudeoChristian tradition a male-created fiction to justify male dominance. The patriarchal god still exists, if only nebulously, but his existence is now affirmed and upheld by women to strengthen their imposition of the school mistress' moral code of fairness, tolerance and equanimity. Fortified by many cups of tea and a little wine, Pym exchanged Milton, propagandist of the School Master God, for a Head Mistress. For Pym, God had not yet become a woman, but Milton had emerged as the Lady of Christ Church.

Two writers more unlike than Milton and Pym could scarcely be found. John Milton, primary propagandist for the Puritan rebellion and defender of regicide, everywhere asserts male privilege. The tentative Miss Pym, though a traditionalist in politics and religion, everywhere questions the premises underlying that privilege. Pym humorously depicted women's heroic efforts to shore up the form of male privilege, even as they despaired that its content was evaporating. In her treatment Milton himself becomes somewhat absurd. Jane, after praising Milton's hymn 'Let us with a gladsome heart', mildly recalls: 'In many ways one dislikes Milton, of course, his treatment of women was not all that it should have been' (JAP 30). The knowledgeable reader is aware of the wink behind Pym's failure to specify the object of Milton's imperative. Subjecting love to reason, woman to man, Milton separated physical attraction from the higher accord of spiritual and intellectual affinity. Pym perceived love as a continuum, its profane manifestations shading into or frequently exchanged with the sacred. The impetus towards caritas might sometimes manifest itself as a desire to bed the girl, as in Rupert's reaction to Penelope in *An Unsuitable Attachment*. While Milton in his male-dominant society feared the incorrect ordering of desire, Pym, in her feminized society feared the failure of desire. To be worthy of the office of high epic/tragic poet, the young Milton believed he must renounce all traffic with the female sex in the maintenance of a perfect chastity. For Pym, becoming a novelist meant embracing amorous experience and recording its impact on the mind and heart. As Henry Harvey complained, Barbara was no simple *ingénue* but a woman whose reason constantly scrutinized her passion (ALTA 49). For all his abstinence, Milton nonetheless married thrice and fathered children. Pym remained single, never experienced motherhood, and deliberately chose a relatively undemanding editorial position to remain free of distraction in her vocation as novelist. Milton inveighed against trivial modem subjects in epic and tragedy. He sought to keep these genres pure of the comic interlude or free from the mixture of the trivial and the commonplace with the heroic. Pym devoted her writing to the depiction of 'the common task, the trivial round' in which average people sometimes display heroism. As she chose her underwear 'with a view to it being seen' (AVPE 33), she kept a meticulous journal which supplied the material for her novels and then assured the journal's being made available to future scholars by willing her papers to the Bodleian Library. These differences between Milton and Pym do not surprise, given the different moments in history occupied by the male and female subjects.

Pym and her characters revealed their devotion in the small 'trivial' acts of cleaning and decorating the church, helping a sick neighbor, visiting an old person, knitting caps for seamen. They sought transcendence through high church ritual (wine and Eros), but they practised a religion implying an immanent deity (tea and Caritas). Milton's personification of the strict schoolmarm enforced the Christian code of morality. Pym's devoted readers will agree that she elucidated the spiritual malaise of English society in the last half of the twentieth century as she chronicled the aging, unsung heroines into whose custodianship the Church has passed.

Notes and references

1. Pym excels in the description of unrequited love. As Nardin points out, Pym showed that "the frustration of desire can be pleasurable"(18). Ackley observes that Pym enjoyed copying out verses about unrequited love and perceived her writing as a kind of therapy (178). Wyatt-Brown perceives the courtly quest as the basis of Pym's relationship with Harvey; Pym shows that unrequited love may be better than a dull marriage, "and much of what Pym's artist-heroines describe ... Is the effect of unre-quited love" (149). Cotsell notes that "Pym registers the comic and touching flow of desire through this dull, respectable church world" (21).
2. See *A Very Private Eye*, eds. Hazel Holt and Hilary Pym, p. 40, 9 May 1934; also Hazel Holt, *A Lot to Ask*.
3. The quotation is from *Genesis* 1:27 in the King James version. Milton, VII, 29-30

says:
    Male he created thee, but thy consort
    Female for race; then bless'd Mankind ...

Works cited

Ackley, Katherine Anne. *The Novels of Barbara Pym*. New York: Garland, 1989.

Burkhart, Charles. *The Pleasure of Miss Pym*. Austin: Univ.Texas Press, 1987.

Benet, Diana. "The Language of Christianity in Pym's Novels." *Thought :a Review of Culture and Idea* **35**, December 1984, p.235.

Corum, Richard. "In White Ink: Paradise Lost and Milton's Ideas of Women." *Milton and the Idea of Woman*, ed. Julia M. Walker. Urbana and Chicago: Univ. Illinois Press, 1988.

Cotsell, Michael. *Barbara Pym*. London: Macmillan, 1989.

Dentith, Simon. *Bakhtinian Thought: an Introductory Reader*. London and New York: Routledge, 1995.

Fergus, Jan."A Glass of Blessings, Jane Austen's Emma, and Barbara Pym's Art of Allusion." In *Independent Women*, ed. Janice Rossen. New York: St. Martin's, 1988.

Frye, Northrop. *Anatomy of Criticism*. New York: Atheneum, 1969.

Gallagher, Philip J. *Milton, the Bible, and Misogyny,* eds. Eugene R. Cunnar and Gail L. Mortimer. Columbia and London: Univ. Missouri Press, 1990.

Gilbert, Sandra and Susanne Gubar. *The Madwoman in the Attic: The Woman Writer and the Nineteenth-Century Literary Imagination.* New Haven and London: Yale UP, 1979.

Halperin, John. "Barbara Pym and the War of the Sexes." In *The Life and Work of Barbara Pym,* ed Dale Salwak. Iowa City: Univ. Iowa Press, 1987.

Holt, Hazel. *A Lot To Ask.* New York: E. P. Dutton, 1991.

Holt, Hazel and Hilary Pym. *A Very Private Eye*. New York: E. P. Dutton, 1984.

Liddell, Robert. *A Mind at Ease.* London: Peter Owen, 1989.

Long, Robert Emmet. *Barbara Pym*. New York: Ungar, 1986.

Milton, John. *Paradise Lost,* ed. Merritt Y. Hughes. New York: Odyssey Press, 1935.

Nardin, Jane. *Barbara Pym*. Boston: Twayne Publishers, 1985.

Paolo, Rosemary de. "You Are What You Drink." *The Barbara Pym Newsletter, II,* 2 Dec. 1987.

Pym, Barbara. *Crampton Hodnet*. New York: E.P. Dutton, 1985.
   Excellent Women. New York: Perennial Library, 1980.
   A Few Green Leaves. New York: Perennial, 1981.
   A Glass of Blessings. New York: Perennial, 1981.
   Jane and Prudence. New York: Perennial, 1982.
   Less Than Angels. New York: Perennial. 1982.
   No Fond Return of Love. New York: Perennial, 1984.
   Quartet in Autumn. New York: Perennial. 1980.
   Some Tame Gazelle. New York: Perennial, 1984.
   The Sweet Dove Died. New York: Perennial, 1980.

An Unsuitable Attachment. New York: Perennial, 1983.

Rossen, Janice. *The World of Barbara Pym.* London: Macmillan, 1987.

Rubenstein, Jill. "Comedy and Consolation in the Novels of Barbara Pym". *Renascence,* 42(3), Spring 1990, pp.173-183.

Salwak, Dale, ed. *The Life and Work of Barbara Pym.* Iowa City: Univ.Iowa Press, 1987.

Snow, Lotus. "Literary Allusions in the Novels". *In* Salwak, Dale, *ibid.*

Strauss-Noll, Mary. "Love and Marriage in the Novels". In Salwak. Dale, ibid.

Weld, Annette. Barbara Pym and the Novel of Manners. London: Macmillan, 1992.

Wittreich, Joseph. *Feminist Milton.* Ithaca: Cornell UP, 1987.

Wyatt-Brown, Anne M. *Barbara Pym: A Critical Biography.* Columbia: Univ. Missouri Press, 1992.

St Benedict in the Precinct:* a Monkish view

Fr. Gabriel Myers, OSB: Monk of St Anselm's Abbey, Washington, DC

I cannot claim to be as good-looking as the lay brother that Leonora glimpsed on Miss Foxe's moving-day. Nor to be as smooth, authoritative, kind and patient as the tour-guide who showed Mildred and Dora around the Abbey on their holiday. I would also say that our monastery is a bit shabbier than that one, with its light and gold and brilliance. But I have lived the life of a Benedictine monk these nine years, and because even my premonastic life was unusually churchy, I feel especially at home in the world of Barbara Pym.

In my late twenties I was the minister of a sad, damp country-church much like the one Piers and Wilmet visit on their weekend with the Talbots. Like Fr Lester I was a bit "higher" than my parishioners. That was actually a Lutheran church, so, like Marius Ransome's roommate and like Adam Prince, I am one who could be said to have "gone over" to the Roman way. Not really because it is a better way than the Lutheran or Anglican.

Perhaps I needed the structure; and I often think that my heart—like Faustina's—remains fiercely Protestant. Once when pressed on this issue, I retorted, "The difference between a Protestant and a Catholic is that a Protestant appreciates hymns for their own sake." I am the monastery organist, and I do love hymns, especially English ones, including Pym favorites like those of Herbert, Keble, and Newman. Mr Valiant-for-Truth's song, "He Who Would Valiant Be," plays a similar role in my life to that of "Lead, Kindly Light" in Barbara's. Perhaps I am even like Ianthe ("very much the canon's daughter this afternoon"), who is offended by Mervyn's parody of "O God Our Help in Ages Past".

I also have the occasional Protestant experience of feeling "churched-out," and sympathize with Barbara's tongue-in-cheek proposal to give up church-going for Lent, but like her I never *quite* have the courage to do so. On bad days I even see myself in Tom Dagnall's organist, Geoffrey Poore, an unbeliever who keeps the job simply for the pleasure of using a fine musical instrument.

Of course, I identify most closely with the main characters of Barbara's novels, even though they are all female and even though I lack the strength of their virtues. For who would *dare* to claim Belinda's contentment or Catherine's independence, Mildred's humility or—I save my favorite for last—Jane's imagination? I am dull by comparison, but the heroines have taught me some powers of observation and expression that have been of great value while living in a monastery.

---

* "Ianthe read on and came to [Father Branche's] own news that he had 'got a church' of his own – 'St Barbara-in-the-Precinct – a very old, almost moribund church, just off High Holborn, very convenient for Gamages." *An Unsuitable Attachment*, chapter 22

For a monastery, leaving aside all its religious dimensions, is a fertile source of the sort of material that Barbara's novels take and refine. There is "such richness!" to use Jane Cleveland's phrase—if only one has the eyes and ears to take it in. I live with eighteen fathers and brothers. It would take the pen of a Jane Austen or Barbara Pym to portray some of the characters (I use the term deliberately) who live in our house. One is so like Mr Collins in *Pride and Prejudice* that really "I could just shake him!" Another monk's conversation is so like that of Miss Bates in full flow that—although, truly, a kinder soul does not exist—one could sympathize with Miss Woodhouse's heartless quip on Box Hill.

The eldest is Fr Urban, aged 87. Rather like Esther Clovis's interrogations on one's field experience, Fr Urban's first question to new acquaintances will always be, "Were *you* at Sant' Anselmo in '37?"

One of my most erudite *confrères* reminds me of Mervyn Cantrell. Not because of gourmet lunches or the coveting of Pembroke tables, but because there is more than a hint of waspishness in his opinions. It must also be admitted that he is somewhat like the Bedes' sewing woman, Miss Prior, in generating *atmosphere*, in eliciting the Aristotelean feelings of pity and fear. "So touchy, so conscious of position, so quick to detect the slightest hint of patronage. One has to be *very* careful" with Brother X.

Fr Joseph has a passionate interest in translating the Hebrew Bible, which reminds me of Gertrude Lydgate's feelings for the Gana verb: "Her white hair stood up on end, for she had been running her fingers through it. The expression on her face was almost one of anguish, her eyes glared through her spectacles." And then the breakthrough:

"Jebel Pingpong! Well I'll be jiggered! Come here *at once*, Father Gemini!"

Fr Joseph has a touching interest in supplying the bird-feeder outside his window. There is a roughly printed sign, "No Crows, small Birds Only." His smile is quite boyish when asked about his birds: in the words of William Caldicote, "I feel like one of those rather dreadful pictures of St Francis, but it's a good feeling, and one does so like to have that."

There is a rich variety of eccentricity in the "bright Christian atmosphere" of our monastery. Dulcie and Viola discuss the implications of that evocative phrase when considering the Anchorage guest-house. Why is one suspicious of such a place? What is one afraid of? "A certain amount of discomfort—and that the Christianity will manifest itself in unpleasant and embarrassing ways," says Viola. But Dulcie is more terribly on target when she adds, "And that one will have to endure the company of those who call themselves Christians. Shall we risk it?"

Mildred Lathbury is aware of the difficulties. "This place gives me a hopeless kind of feeling," she says in the self-service cafeteria. "One wouldn't believe there could be so many people, and one must love them all." I tend to sympathize with Mrs Bonner's rather shocked response, looking up from her chocolate trifle, "Oh, I don't think the Commandment is meant to be taken as literally as that." And yet that is exactly what one must manage to try to do if one is to grow in a monastery, or anywhere.

The ideal of loving one's neighbor is sounded by Nicholas Cleveland when his wife shows distress over the small-mindedness of their parochial church council.

> 'I didn't think it would be like this,' Jane lamented. 'I thought people in the country were somehow noble, through contact with the earth and nature,' she smiled, 'and all the time they're worrying about petty details like water-tanks and magazine covers – like people in the suburbs.'
>
> 'We must accept people as we find them and do the best we can,' said Nicholas in too casual a tone to sound priggish.

I submit that the monastic task, when one moves beyond the romantic illusions that surround "the call of the cloister," is largely a matter of risking the company of those who call themselves Christians. I do not mean to be reductive or cynical, for I *think* that the "spiritual" and the "earthly," the "trivial" and the "profound," are so intricately woven together that it nearly impossible to separate the strands. For this lurching union of opposites, this unsuitable attachment, Barbara Pym had a unique, subtle, and totally original understanding. By using her outlook I have been better able to manage my own monastic experience.

On the wall over my bed hangs a framed black-and-white postcard of Finstock Church. (Barbara's sister suggests that its noble 19th-century simplicity was rather spoiled by the pretentious chancel added in 1902, in memory of the vicar's mother—but I, sentimentally, like it just the way it is.) The photograph is there to remind me of the diary entry in *A Very Private Eye* dated 30th July 1976. Note the composure and serenity of this passage which was written after thirteen years of publishers' rejections. Barbara had no way of foreseeing the reocognition that would come six months later. For me this is a perfect encapsulation of Barbara's personality, her modesty and strength.

> Philip Larkin came to tea, then we walked up to the church to see the T.S. Eliot memorial. So two great poets and one minor novelist came for a brief moment (as it were) together. What is the point of saying (as if for posterity) what Philip is *like*. He is so utterly what he is in his letters and poems... 'Life at graduate level,' as he once said about my novel *No Fond Return of Love*.

The phrase "life at graduate level" is unexplained, but its meaning is suggested by another Larkin description of Barbara's work:[1]

> In all her writing I find a continual perceptive attention to detail, and a steady background of rueful yet courageous acceptance of things, which I find more relevant to life as most of us have to live it, than spies coming in from the cold.

I believe that Barbara achieved this degree of acceptance with the help of prayer, and 1 think prayer had this power for her because she was so unpretentious about it. Her characters certainly are, and they are more encouraging to my own feeble efforts than more overtly pious testimonials.

Think of Jane Cleveland trying (and failing) to realize the Presence of God in the vicarage drawing-room, because she is more conscious of the sound of Mrs Glaze doing the washing-up in the back kitchen. Or Mildred Lathbury, trying to deal with her very genuine grief after Rocky's departure. She goes into St Mary's and tries to draw comfort from the Victorian atmosphere, until interrupted by Miss Statham with Brasso and polishing cloth in hand. "Just thinking something over," Mildred explains. Or Catherine – not a regular churchgoer – lighting a candle for Tom's safety, and wondering whether stilted, archaic language is necessary in addressing God. She, like Mildred, is caught by an excellent woman.

'I was only just ...' she had been going to say 'looking around,' as if she were in a shop but stopped herself in time.

I should think these fumbling efforts are recognizable to anyone who has ever tried to pray.

I am fond of the description of Tom Dagnall's practice of going into the church for a half-hour or so "not exactly to meditate or pray, but to wander in random fashion around the aisles, letting his thoughts dwell on various villagers." He rightly recognizes that this is a kind of prayer, "like bringing them into the church, which so few of them actually visited." It is a meaningful and generous approach to pastoral care, in an age when the clergy's efforts can seem ineffectual.

Then there is the prayer of praise, thanks, delight – perhaps the purest form because the least self-conscious. It is the kind that Belinda experiences at the end of that terribly full afternoon of grim dough-rolling, aching back, Mrs Ramage, and Bishop Grote's ghastly proposal, when the ravioli paste is (at last!) the consistency of the finest chamois leather.

There is a hint or foreshadowing in this scene from Barbara's first novel of her own way of dealing with her years in the wilderness. Belinda's behavior suggests the internal resources that Barbara drew on: integrity, clear-mindedness, and delight in excellence. In fact, it seems to indicate the great monastic virtue of perseverance. The Gospel says, "the one who perseveres to the end will be saved". That can be rather a struggle. I experienced this in various delays and disappointments before arriving at my final (or solemn) profession in 1994.

My profession day at the monastery was one of almost perfect happiness, not so different from the final chapter of *A Glass of Blessings,* or Harriet's quotation to the Archdeacon, "'Behold, how good and joyful a thing is it, brethren, to dwell together in unity'. The psalm, you know ..."

I carried in my breast pocket a talisman that Hilary Walton had sent me. It is a New Testament, $2^1/2$ x 4-inch, in a burgundy-colored binding with a ribbon marker, published by Oxford University Press, in the Authorized Version. While in good condition, it clearly shows signs of use; the spine has ridges from the book's having lain flat, and the gilt edge of the pages has become dull. I suspect it was bumped around a bit while being carried in one of those large black day-handbags that Barbara teased herself about. Her name and the date she began using it are marked on the inside front cover – 'Barbara Pym, Christmas 1951' – with a whimsical little asterisk that might represent the Epiphany star.

There are a few pencil-marked passages and a few references jotted down on the inside back cover. The first of them seems to have been used on one of all those Sundays after Trinity, and is from the *Letter to the Romans.* It is an amazingly suitable text for Barbara's own lifestory and a wonderfully encouraging reminder for mine. *Romans* 8.18:

> For I reckon that the sufferings of this present time are not worthy to be compared with the glory which shall be revealed in us.

Barbara was not preachy, but she clearly believed that life has a larger pattern than the individual happy or sad patches that we experience in the present moment. She did not get stuck in those patches as I sometimes do. Without minimizing life's difficulties, she shows us what the right true end of living should be. This is especially clear in the closing lines of her novels: a full life after all, a sense of the overwhelming richness of life, a realization of life's infinite possibilities for change, a love affair which need not necessarily be an unhappy one.

To me, these lines are a little touch of heaven.

References

1. Thwaite, Anthony, ed. *Selected Letters of Philip Larkin*. NY: Farrar, Straus, 1992, p. 376.

At ease with ladies:
Barbara Pym and the Clergy

Kate Charles

Barbara Pym's first published novel, *Some Tame Gazelle*, famously opens with the new curate coming to supper – a fresh, funny, typically Barbara Pym scene. It signals an interest in the clergy which was to be reflected in almost every book she wrote.

In her world, the Church of England looms large, and I suppose this is one reason why I love her books so much, along with the understated humour, the deep vein of irony, and her very particular gift for observation.

Her novels feature in detail not only the Church, but also curates, clergy wives, even clergy housekeepers.

In *No Fond Return of Love*, Aylwin Forbes ponders:

> No doubt, like all men connected with the Church – his brother Neville included – the organist would be at ease with ladies. He could see the phrase – At Ease with Ladies – as the title of a novel or even a biography.

In her last novel, *A Few Green Leaves*, Pym repeats the phrase, and the sentiment:

> Emma had been thinking that no man would dare to attend the sale but then she realized that, of course, there could be exceptions. A former Anglican priest might well have the sort of courage required for the occasion and Adam, so very much at ease with ladies, obviously came into this category.

I will consider Barbara Pym's clergy in relation to the women in their lives: their wives, their sisters, and above all those worthy parish women who support, cherish and pamper them and – heaven help them – even fall in love with them; women of the sort described in *Excellent Women* as 'holy fowls', women like Harriet and Belinda Bede.

By necessity, we'll be looking at male clergy only. Of course there *were* no women clergy when Pym was writing, and I don't think she really envisioned a time when that might happen. In *A Glass of Blessings*, her narrator Wilmet observes:

> 'I think clergymen are always surrounded at functions like these.'
>
> 'Yes,' Sir Denbigh agreed. 'It makes one wonder whether it would really be proper to admit women to Holy Orders. Is it likely that a woman would be surrounded by men at a parish gathering and would it be seemly if she were?'
>
> 'I suppose one visualises rather plain-looking middle-aged and elderly women taking Orders,' said Miss Prideaux.
>
> 'Surrounded by men of the same type or perhaps not surrounded at all?' said Sir Denbigh. 'Yes, I see your point – perhaps it would be like that.

I will concentrate on Pym's Anglican clergymen. She *did* write about a few sinister Romans, and even a non-conformist or two, but it was the Church of England that she inhabited and loved, even as she described it in *Crampton Hodnet*, when her curate Mr Latimer takes Evensong:

> Yes, this was the Church of England, his flock, thought Mr Latimer, a collection of old women, widows and spinsters, and one young man not quite right in the head.

Curates in Barbara Pym novels are almost always described as good-looking. They are, in fact, much of a type – handsome, a bit pompous, taking themselves rather too seriously. There must be something about the type that appeals to Miss Harriet Bede in *Some Tame Gazelle*, as her abiding interest, and life-long hobby, is cherishing – and feeding – curates. There have been many of them over the years, apparently interchangeable and all equally doted upon, though the paler the better. Her sister Belinda is bemused by all of this: 'How many curates would starve and die were it not for the Harriets of this world?' she thinks. And when they have reason to visit the curate's lodgings:

> This was quite a nice room, not as meanly furnished as Harriet could have wished, though Belinda was relieved that they did not have to provide the curate with furniture as well as food.

The current curate, and thus the object of Harriet's interest, is called Edgar Donne. His maternal grandfather was a bishop, which seems to give him an added lustre, but he is as pompous and self-involved as any other Pym curate. His Christmas gift to the Bede sisters is a photograph of himself.

Mr Donne breaks the mould, though, when he does something that none of Harriet's curates has done before: he decides to get married. Or rather, the decision is made for him when Olivia Berridge, the blue-stocking niece of the Vicar's wife Agatha, takes matters out of his hands and proposes to him. Predictably, this does not go down well with Harriet Bede.

> 'It's much better for a curate not to marry. Just imagine, a married curate,' said Harriet in disgust.

But it seems that Mr Donne has done rather well for himself in Olivia. The parish gets its first glimpse of her at a party to celebrate their engagement:

> It was obvious that she would take care of him, not letting him cast a clout too soon. She would probably help with his sermons too, and embellish them with quotations rarer than her husband, with his Third Class in Theology, could be expected to know. A helpmeet indeed.

Stephen Latimer, the new curate who arrives at the beginning of *Crampton Hodnet,* is auburn-haired, tall and broad-shouldered, charming and personable, in a rather facile way. It is arranged that he shall have a room in the North Oxford house of Miss Doggett, a formidable spinster, and her meek companion Miss Jessie Morrow. From the outset it is clear that Miss Doggett is no Harriet Bede:

> 'I don't think I could spend my time running up and down stairs with glasses of hot milk and poached eggs.'

At first Mr Latimer is circumspect and cautious:

He believed that he was going to be very comfortable here. Of course Miss Doggett made a fuss of him, as all women did, but he rather liked this, as long as he wasn't expected to give anything in return except the politeness and charm which came to him without effort. And, after all, what else could he be expected to give to an old woman of seventy? He liked the companion too, an amusing, sensible little woman, who wasn't likely to throw her arms round his neck, for poor Mr Latimer had experienced even that.

But quickly Mr Latimer develops a friendship with Miss Morrow, under Miss Doggett's very nose and without her being in the least aware of it. Mr Latimer and Miss Morrow go for a walk on a Sunday afternoon, resulting in his missing Evensong, which makes a bond between them that has interesting consequences.

It was amazing how, even with the restraining presence of Miss Doggett, they always seemed to be talking about love, or what passed for love in a circle consisting of clergymen and spinsters.

Thinking things over in bed that night, Mr Latimer came to the conclusion that he might have to take some action in the matter himself, if only for his own safety and peace of mind. After all, he was thirty-five years old, old enough to know his own mind and yet not so old that he would behave as those elderly clergymen one read about in the cheaper daily papers, who married a servant or a chorus girl of eighteen. He was a man of private means, good-looking and charming. It was obvious that he could never expect to have much peace until he was safely married. Besides, there was something comforting about the idea of having a wife, a helpmeet, somebody who would keep the others off and minister to his needs without being as fussy as Miss Doggett was. Some nice, sensible woman, not too young.
It was then that it occurred to him that he might do worse than marry Miss Morrow.

He seizes the opportunity to carry this plan through one evening when Miss Doggett is out.

'Oh, Miss Morrow – Janie,' he burst out suddenly.
'My name isn't Janie.
'Well, it's something beginning with J,' he said impatiently. It was annoying to be held up by such a triviality. What did it matter what her name was at this moment?

Things go downhill from there, and Miss Morrow sensibly refuses him. By the end of the novel, Mr Latimer has met someone far more suitable while on holiday in Paris, the younger daughter of Lord Pimlico, no less, and has become engaged to her.

In *A Glass of Blessings* we encounter the beautiful Marius Ransome, the new curate at St Luke's. Wilmet Forsyth, the first-person narrator of this book, describes him:

His christian names – Marius Lovejoy – and the first glimpse of him earlier in the evening had led me to expect somebody handsome, but even so the impact of his good looks was quite startling. He was certainly very handsome indeed, with his dark wavy hair and large brown eyes. The bones in his face were well defined and his expression serious.

Predictably, Mr Ransome is charming to the ladies of the parish, and is much admired. Because there is no room at the clergy house, though, it is necessary for him – like Mr Latimer – to lodge with someone in the parish. In this case it is old Mrs Beamish, a dragon of a woman, and her dowdy spinster daughter Mary. Not much of a danger for the beautiful Mr Ransome there, you might think. Then old Mrs Beamish dies, leaving Mr Ransome a legacy of five hundred pounds, and he moves out of the Beamish house to lodge with Father Edwin Sainsbury, a friend from theological college days. Father Sainsbury has leanings towards Rome, and the parishioners at St Luke's worry that Mr Ransome might be swayed to follow him in leaving the Church of England. But Mr Ransome surprises everyone by proposing to Mary Beamish. Mary herself tells Wilmet about the proposal – how Marius, as she now calls him, arrived on the new motor scooter which he's bought with her mother's legacy, and asked her to marry him.

> I could hardly confess my first reaction to her news, which was the perhaps typically feminine one of astonishment that such a good-looking man as Marius Ransome should want to marry anyone so dim and mousy as Mary Beamish. But as soon as I pushed aside this unworthy thought I realized what a good wife she would make for a clergyman, especially one as unstable as Marius appeared to be. Mary was obviously just the person he needed to steady him, and the novelty and responsibility of marriage would surely take his mind off Rome.

Another curate making a passing appearance is Basil Branche in *An Unsuitable Attachment*. He had once served as curate to the father of Ianthe Broome, and she recognises 'the dark handsome young man in the opposite corner' as she is travelling in Rome with a parish party. He tells them that his health has broken down and he has been ordered to take a long holiday in the South of France or Italy.

> 'How lucky that you were able to arrange it,' said Ianthe, not in the least sarcastically.
>
> 'Yes, a most extraordinary thing happened. I was glancing through the personal column of the *Church Times* when I saw an advertisement for "a curate in poor health" – those were the very words – to accompany two elderly ladies on an Italian tour, all expenses paid.'

The ladies in question are, of course, the Bede sisters, and we are given a delightful glimpse of Harriet in her old age, still pursuing her favourite hobby.

> 'There you are,' she cried out in a ringing tone. 'I've been looking for you everywhere. You went out without your scarf and you know how treacherous these Italian nights are.'

Soon Harriet takes Basil Branche away.

He was like some tame animal being led away, thought Penelope scornfully. She didn't see how anyone could take him seriously, not even a clergyman's daughter, who might be thought to have to make do with her father's curates.

Now let us consider a Bishop. Every bishop was a curate once, and Theodore Grote was, long ago, one of Harriet's beloved curates.

[Harriet] had no difficulty in recalling him as one of the most sought-after curates in the history of the Church of England. In his heyday there had been quite a procession of doting women towards his lodgings, carrying cooked pheasants and chickens, iced cakes, even jellies in basins.

He has now risen to be the Bishop of Mbawawa, in Africa.

Dear Theo, he had certainly done splendid work among the natives, at least, that was what everyone said, although nobody seemed to know exactly what it was that he had done.

Theo Grote's appearance in the village causes quite a stir, not least amongst the ladies of the parish. But Theo Grote has changed.

Could a beautiful curate have grown into this tall, stringy-looking man, with a yellow, leathery complexion? His expression reminded Belinda of a sheep more than anything; his face was long, his forehead domed and his head bald. He was even rather toothy, a thing that Harriet abhorred.

The parishioners get their first glimpse of Bishop Grote at a gathering at the parish hall, where he lectures to them about his life in Africa.

'I dare say some of you would like to hear what the language sounds like,' said the Bishop, 'so I am going to sing a few verses of a song which the Mbawawa adapt to many occasions, birth, marriage, death, all the great events in this mortal life have their own form of it.' ...
    The voice of the Bishop rang out through the hall in song. Many handkerchiefs were taken out hastily, especially among the younger members of the audience, for the noise which filled the hall was quite unexpected. Even Belinda, who had heard the Bishop sing as a curate, was a little unprepared.

Belinda is equally unprepared for what happens next. Bishop Theo comes to call, and it is Belinda that he wants to see, rather than Harriet.

'I think I had better speak more plainly,' the Bishop went on. 'I am asking you to marry me.'
    There was a short but awkward silence, and then Belinda heard herself stammering out the first words that came into her head. 'Oh, but I couldn't.'
    'My dear, you are equal to being the wife of a bishop,' he said kindly, making a movement towards her. 'You need have no fears on that account. When I was a younger man I held views about the celibacy of the clergy, young curates often do, you know,' he smiled indulgently, 'it is a kind of protection, if you know what I mean.'

Belinda turns him down, but it isn't long until he finds someone more willing – one of the dim village spinsters, whom he runs into in the Army and Navy Store when he is stocking up on supplies before his return to Africa. I can just imagine him ticking the items off his list: mosquito netting, water sterilising tablets, wife ... The last we hear of him, Belinda is speculating about his future.

'Of course, he won't be Bishop of Mbawawa all his life. I suppose he may retire and write a book about his experiences. They often do, don't they?'

'With cassock and surplice in Mbawawa-land,' retorted Edith. 'Yes, one knows the kind of thing only too well.'

While the typical Pym curate is good-looking and self-centred, the typical Pym vicar is a celibate Anglo-Catholic. The celibacy of the clergy is a big issue with Barbara Pym; her characters are constantly discussing the topic in relation to various clergy, and as an abstract principle. Even those clergy who are married, like Mark Ainger in *An Unsuitable Attachment*, sometimes wonder about it. His wife Sophia, a woman who seems more devoted to her cat Faustina than to her husband, tells him that Ianthe Broome is to marry.

'Surely that can't be a good thing.'

'No, better not to marry,' he agreed, but was thinking not of Ianthe and the young man from the library, but rather of the clergy in general and perhaps at that moment of himself in particular. How could Faustina's hairs have got here, he had asked himself at the early Mass that morning, seeing them on the fair linen cloth on the altar.

Nicholas Cleveland, husband of the eponymous Jane of *Jane and Prudence,* has second thoughts on the subject when Jane speaks out of turn at a PCC meeting and embarrasses him.

She would never learn when not to speak, he thought, with rather less affectionate tolerance than usual. Not for the first time he began to consider that there was, after all, something to be said for the celibacy of the clergy.

But when the vicar in question is unmarried and good-looking, speculation reaches fever-pitch, as in *Excellent Women.* Julian Malory is the vicar of St Mary's, Pimlico. Aged about forty, he lives with his sister Winifred. They have both become friends with Mildred Lathbury, the narrator of the book. Mildred, whose father was a canon, is active in parish affairs.

With my parochial experience, I know myself to be capable of dealing with most of the stock situations or even the great moments of life – birth, marriage, death, the successful jumble sale, the garden fete spoiled by bad weather . 'Mildred is such a help to her father,' people used to say after my mother died.

So it is natural that she and Julian should become friends, and that people should discuss his marital status with her. Mrs Morris, the cleaning woman, says:

'It isn't natural for a man not to be married.'

'Clergymen don't always want to,' I explained, 'or they think it better that they shouldn't.'

Helena Napier, Mildred's worldly neighbour, says:

'He isn't married then? One of those ... I mean,' she added apologetically as if she had said something that might offend me, 'one of the kind who don't marry?'

'Well, he isn't married and as he's about forty I dare say he won't now.' I seemed to have spent so much time lately in talking about the celibacy of the clergy in general and Julian Malory in particular that I was a little tired of the subject.

'That's just when they break out,' laughed Mrs Napier. 'I always imagine that clergymen need wives to help them with their parish work, but I suppose most of his congregation are devout elderly women with nothing much to do, so that's all right. Holy fowl, you know.'

Mildred herself observes:

There was usually something rather forbidding about [Julian's] manner so that women did not tend to fuss over him as they might otherwise have done. ... I suppose he was neither so handsome nor so conceited as to pretend a belief in celibacy as a protection, and I did not really know his views on the matter. It seemed a comfortable arrangement for the brother and sister to live together, and perhaps it is more suitable that a High Church clergyman should remain unmarried, that there should be a biretta in the hall rather than a perambulator.

There are many in the parish who believe, secretly, that Julian and Mildred will marry. Julian depends a great deal on Mildred. When he is attempting to distemper a room in the vicarage:

The sound of women's voices raised in what seemed to be a lamentation led me to a large room on the top floor, where I found Julian Malory sitting on top of a step-ladder, holding a brush and wearing an old cassock streaked with yellow distemper. Standing around him were [several women of the parish]. They were all staring at a wall which Julian had apparently just finished. ...

'Oh, Mildred,' Julian waved his brush towards me in a despairing gesture, showering everybody with drops of distemper, 'do come to the rescue!'

Mildred, along with the rest of the parish, is amazed when Julian becomes engaged to Allegra Gray, the attractive clergy widow who has moved into the refurbished flat at the top of the vicarage. Mildred insists that people need not feel sorry for her – marrying Julian was not what she wanted for herself. Allegra Gray invites her out to lunch for a heart-to-heart talk.

She was trying to tell me how glad and relieved she was that I didn't mind too much when I must surely have wanted to marry Julian myself.

'Oh, no, of course I don't mind,' I said. 'We have always been good friends, but there's never been any question of anything else, anything more than friendship.'

... it had not occurred to me that anyone might think I was in love with Julian. But there it was, the old obvious solution, presentable unmarried clergyman and woman interested in good works.

Then it all ends in tears, as Julian discovers the true duplicitous nature of Allegra Gray, and arrives on Mildred's doorstep shortly after a tearful Winifred.

I went down and found Julian Malory outside the door. He was hatless and had flung round his shoulders one of those black speckled mackintoshes which seem to be worn only by clergymen. He looked worried and upset. ...

'The engagement is broken off,' said Julian flatly. ...

'Perhaps clergymen shouldn't marry,' I said, realizing that Julian was a free man again and that we ladies of the parish need no longer think of ourselves as the rejected ones. But the thought did not, at that moment, arouse any very great enthusiasm in me.

Barbara Pym waits several years, until *A Glass of Blessings*, to give us another glimpse of Julian Malory, and we discover that his circumstances have not changed.

Julian Malory was a dark, rather good looking man in his late forties. There was something about him that reminded me a little of our own Father Ransome, though perhaps it was nothing more subtle than the angle of his biretta. While he was preaching I found myself wondering whether he was married or not, until I remembered Miss Prideaux having said that he lived with his sister.

He also makes a brief appearance in *An Unsuitable Attachment*, where he is compared unfavourably to Mark Ainger, and described as 'one of those unfortunate men who dislike their neighbours even more than they dislike themselves'. Poor Julian.

And poor Neville Forbes, the vicar in *No Fond Return of Love*. The book opens with his brother Aylwin, an academic, preparing to present a paper on 'Some problems of an editor'; but I suspect that Barbara Pym is more interested in 'Some problems of a celibate priest.'

Neville's problems have to do with women, and it is no wonder: Father Forbes is handsome enough to be a curate – he is described as 'exceptionally good-looking'; similar in features to ... his brother Aylwin, 'but less care-worn, the hair fairer and curling round the temples like an angel in an Italian Renaissance painting'. Dulcie Mainwaring visits Neville's church and sees a woman rushing into the church in tears. She talks to Neville's housekeeper:

'He's not married?' asked Dulcie boldly.

'Oh, no!' The woman looked surprised at the question, as if Dulcie ought to have known that he was not married. 'But of course a good-looking man like that would have his difficult moments - only to be expected, seeing what women are, too. ...

Dulcie could not but agree. ... It looked rather as if Neville Forbes had got himself involved with some woman, perhaps a young Sunday School teacher, or even a married woman._

Later Dulcie tells her friend Viola about what has happened.

'I don't suppose it was anything much,' said Viola in her usual damping way. 'The clergy are always having women make scenes over them – one reads about it in the papers nearly every day. ... Clergymen are rather at the mercy of women, aren't they; all this popping into church at odd times.'

Dulcie and Viola return to the church and hears more details from the indiscreet housekeeper.

'That's right, dear,' she said. 'She fell in love with Father Forbes. Well, she's not the first to do that – he is good-looking, you know ... But he's a celibate, of course.' Here her tone took on a sterner, more vigorous note.

Dulcie asks what happened:

'Oh, she said she loved him – waylaid him one night after Benediction – a week or two ago, now ... she followed him back to the vicarage ... I heard her voice in the hall, or rather his voice.'
'What was he saying?' Viola asked.
'Oh, I didn't hear, really,' said the housekeeper. 'I suppose the kind of things men do say when women get troublesome in that way.'
Are there then 'things' that men invariably say in such situations? Dulcie wondered. Does it happen all that often? Perhaps more to the clergy than to other men, and perhaps they, being practised speakers anyway, would find the 'things' easier to bring out.

In confusion, Neville flees from his London parish and goes to stay with his mother, an eccentric woman who runs a guest house in a North Devon resort. But she is less than thrilled to be landed with Neville and his problems.

Neville could hardly even be called upon to wait at table, for he insisted on wearing his cassock all the time, and even had he worn only an ordinary dark suit and his clerical collar he would still have looked a little unusual, taking the dishes from the hatch and bringing them to the tables. Besides, people just did not like a clergyman wandering about in a hotel: it was to be hoped that he would have gone back before the Easter visitors arrived. ...
Although he had said nothing about his reasons for coming, Mrs Forbes guessed that it must be, in her own words, 'trouble with a woman', for it had happened before. What began as a pleasant friendship between priest and parish worker all too often blossomed – or should one say degenerated ? – into love on the woman's part. And even now Neville seemed quite unable to deal with it. He should either marry or go into a monastery, thought Mrs Forbes firmly, though even marriage would not prevent the female members of his flock from falling in love with him.

Then Neville tells his mother:

'It may be that I shall have to marry her ... I mean that it might make things easier all round, and I dare say she'd make quite a good wife.'
'I thought you didn't hold with marriage.'
'I don't really, for a priest, but there could be situations where one might have to sacrifice one's principles for the happiness of another person.'

Another handsome celibate clergyman who toys with the idea of marriage is Father David Lydell, in *Quartet in Autumn*. When Letty, one of the eponymous quartet, goes to visit her friend Marjorie in the country, she finds that Marjorie is well acquainted with, and interested in, the new vicar.

The Reverend David Lydell (he liked to be called 'Father') was a tall dark man in his middle forties who certainly looked good in his vestments. Nice for Marjorie to have an interesting new vicar, Letty thought, generously indulgent.

Later, when he visits Marjorie:

Father Lydell, obviously with no evening meal of his own in view, lingered on, so that Marjorie had to ask him to stay to supper.

But it would seem that Marjorie is not the only woman in the parish interested in David Lydell.

'This is one of Father Lydell's favourite dishes,' said Beth, bringing a covered casserole to the table. Poulet niçoise – I hope you like it.'
'Oh, yes,' Letty murmured, remembering the times she had eaten poulet niçoise at Marjorie's house. Had David Lydell gone all round the village sampling the cooking of the unattached women before deciding which one to settle with?

Then disaster strikes. Marjorie rings to tell Letty that the engagement had been broken off.

'Beth Doughty,' Marjorie wailed. 'And I had no idea ...'
For a moment Letty couldn't remember who Beth Doughty was, then it came back to her. ... the efficient woman who knew the kind of food David Lydell liked and remembered his passion for Orvieto. There was something shocking in the idea of two women competing for the love of a clergyman with the lure of food and wine, but the whole pattern slotted into place.
Letty began to wonder whether Beth Doughty might not also be rejected in her turn, whether no woman would succeed in bringing David Lydell to the point of marriage, but she did not say anything of this.

Atypically, Father Oswald Thames, in *A Glass of Blessings,* is not a handsome clergyman in his middle years. In spite of the fact that he has exquisite taste, and, like David Lydell, holidays in Italy, he proves himself, every time he opens his mouth, to be a bit of an old windbag. He is described as 'a tall scraggy old man with thick white hair and a beaky nose' – not exactly the sort of thing to set feminine hearts aflutter. That does not mean that he is above using what leverage he has on the women in his congregation. He writes in the parish magazine of his difficulties at the clergy house, now that his housekeeper is retiring.

Now we are really in the soup! Prayers, please, and practical help. Isn't there some good woman ... who would feel drawn to do really Christian work and look after Father Bode and myself? We can just about boil an egg between us!

Wilmet Forsyth reads his plea as she sits in the church, and he appears before her.

Father Thames hovered over me like a great bird. 'Do you know,' he went on, 'I thought for one moment when I saw you sitting there reading the parish paper that you might be the answer to prayer.' ...
'I've just been reading about Mrs Greenhill leaving,' I said. 'I do hope you've got somebody else to keep house for you?'

'No, alas, not yet. That's why I was thinking how wonderful it would be if you, reading my *cri de coeur*' – he paused and gave me a most appealing look. I wondered whether many men, perhaps the clergy especially, went about cajoling or bullying women into being the answer to prayer. I supposed that the technique must often be successful.

Successful enough for Tom Dagnall to repeat it. Tom, the middle-aged rector in *A Few Green Leaves,* is described as 'a tall man, austerely good-looking, but his brown eyes lacked the dog-like qualities so often associated with that colour'. He has been left in the lurch, as he considers, by his sister Daphne, who has decamped to greener pastures – Birmingham – to live with a friend. He writes in the parish magazine:

> It is often said that the best chefs are men, but I cannot claim to belong to that noble and skilled fraternity, so I am going to throw myself on the mercy of the ladies and put my trust in their kind hearts and culinary skills. I am asking you to take pity on me and invite me to an occasional meal in your homes, to share in whatever you are having yourselves, a simple family meal, eaten in congenial company.

One of the women – perhaps the only one – to fall for this line is Emma Howick, a newcomer to the village. Emma isn't really a church-goer, but she likes Tom and feels a bit sorry for him. He is more than willing to take advantage of her, from the very first:

> It occurred to him that even if she didn't come to Evensong, she might be helpful in other ways. She might be a good typist, though he could hardly ask her to do such menial work, or even be expert at deciphering Elizabethan handwriting, a skill none of his willing lady helpers possessed.

Note the plural here. Tom, it would seem, is a user of women. His passion in life is local history, and he seems obsessed by such trivia as the location of a deserted mediaeval village, and the ancient custom of 'burying in wool'. The ladies of the parish help him by copying inscriptions from old tomb stones and poring through old parish records, and on the domestic side he is looked after by his sister Daphne. Tom was once married, but his wife died. He tells Emma about his late wife.

> Tom went on talking about the time after Laura had died, and even seemed to be making excuses for not having married again.
> 'I didn't seem to have the chance, or meet anyone suitable.' He must have been aware how feeble he sounded. As if a man, especially one connected with the church, couldn't meet a woman if he had a mind to, however much hemmed in by a sister!
> 'But people in your parish – in London and here – there must have been ...' Emma protested.
> 'Oh, there were, of course. Every church has plenty of eligible women, but somehow ...'

Tom, by Emma's own observation, could not be called dynamic. Although he is personable and good looking, people like Emma's mother can't help thinking of him as 'poor Tom'.

'Ineffectual' was the word that sprang to mind when she thought of Tom – not even capable of locating the site of that ridiculous deserted medieval village in the woods ... And not all that efficient in the running of his church, either. Beatrix found herself remembering certain lapses of detail ... Christmas decorations still up on the first Sunday after Epiphany, daffodils on the altar at Quinquagesima – surely incorrect? – which Tom ought to have picked up but probably hadn't even noticed. But of course he had lost his wife, one must remember that, and was saddled with the unfortunate Daphne. Poor Tom – and poor Daphne. Definitely poor Daphne.

Daphne herself wonders about this:

All these years making a home for somebody who hardly even noticed that she was there! Heather always said it had been a mistake, this rushing to make a home for Tom when Laura died. If it hadn't been for her doing this, Tom might have married again, probably would have done, seeing the way women went after the clergy. Had she protected him from a grisly fate or stood in the way of his happiness? She would never know.

The reader will never know either, though there is some suggestion at the very end of this, her last novel, that Emma and Tom will get together. I'm not sure whether this is a good thing or a bad thing, at least for Emma. For 'poor Tom', surely, it would be a great relief, after Daphne's defection.

Another vicar and his sister appear, intriguingly, off-stage in *No Fond Return of Love*. When Dulcie goes to visit her Aunt Hermione, she finds her on the phone, discussing the fact that the vicar's sister, who has always kept house for him, has died, leaving the vicar adrift. Later in the book, Dulcie calls again, and discovers that Aunt Hermione herself has stepped into the breach:

'I insisted on an engagement ring,' said Hermione, stretching out her hand the better to display the gold ring set with three diamonds. 'People will gossip, you know, and I've been doing so much popping in and out of the vicarage lately.'

She explains to Dulcie:

'I gave him a week or two – poor man, he soon got into a fine old muddle! Then one day I thought I'd take him by surprise, so I popped round one morning and what do you think he was doing? Trying to wash his surplices! He was worried because they didn't seem as white as they ought to be.'

And the rest, as they say, is history!

That leads us neatly into the category of married clergymen. There *are* a few in Pym, mostly on the side-lines. Even in books in which they feature as important characters, they take second place to their more interesting wives. There is, for example, Nicholas Cleveland, husband of Jane in *Jane and Prudence.* Jane is a wonderful character – scatty, disorganised, and imaginative. Nicholas, in contrast, is a mild-mannered fellow, Low-to-middle in churchmanship, vague and kindly, somewhat otherworldly, unambitious, given to childish delight in animal-shaped soaps. He has the rather far-fetched idea of growing his own tobacco as an economy measure, and ends up drying the leaves from the clothes airer in the vicarage kitchen.

Then there is Mark Ainger, in *An Unsuitable Attachment*. Mark is married to Sophia, and the word that best describes him is 'remote'. There is a mention of

> Mark's eyes, which were also blue, but with that remote expression sometimes found in the eyes of sailors or explorers. Although invariably kind and courteous he had the air of seeming not to be particularly interested in human beings — a somewhat doubtful quality in a parish priest, though it had its advantages.

Sophia's sister Penelope finds this as well:

> Penelope did not answer. Her brother-in-law, with his remote good looks, never seemed quite real to her. She found it difficult to imagine him getting something for supper.

Even odder and more remote is Archdeacon Henry Hoccleve, the vicar of the parish in *Some Tame Gazelle*. Henry is difficult: irascible, learned, quirky, unpersonable, not at all accommodating or kindly. He is larger than life, much given to wandering about the churchyard among the tombs, declaiming melancholic 18th century poetry. Henry is married to Agatha, a formidable woman whose father was a bishop. But the main woman in his life is Belinda Bede, who has cherished an unrequited love for him for over thirty years, since their days together at university. Occasionally she allows herself to think wistfully of how things might have been, as when looking at wool in the wool shop:

> Here was an admirable clerical grey. Such nice soft wool too ... would she ever dare to knit a pullover for the Archdeacon? ... She might send it anonymously, or give it to him casually, as if it had been left over from the Christmas charity parcel. Surely that would be quite seemly, unless of course it might appear rather ill-mannered?
> 'This is a lovely clerical grey,' said Miss Jenner, as if sensing her thoughts. 'I've sold quite a lot of this to various ladies round here – especially in Father Plowman's parish.'

Father Plowman is the good-looking celibate Anglo-Catholic vicar of the adjoining parish.

Belinda decides to buy the wool.

> After all, she might make a jumper for herself, now that she came to think of it she was certain that she would, either that or something else equally safe and dull. When we grow older we lack the fine courage of youth, and even an ordinary task like making a pullover for somebody we love or used to love seems too dangerous to be undertaken.

Oh, dear. Things get more interesting for Belinda later in the book, when Agatha goes off to a German spa to take the waters, and Belinda finds the courage to pamper Henry a bit. But we know as well as she does that nothing will ever come of it.

I'd like to return to my title, 'At Ease with Ladies', and consider its implications. My conclusion is that Barbara Pym, in her novels, treated the clergy as a sort of third gender – not women, but not exactly real men, either. References abound, and I'll give just a few. Take, for example, Julian Malory, when he experiences difficulty with the distempering:

> 'I suppose I am not to be considered as a normal man,' said Julian, taking off his yellow-streaked cassock and draping it over the step-ladder, 'and yet I do have these manly feelings.'

Later, when Mildred and her friend Dora see Julian holding hands with Allegra Gray:

> 'It looks odd to see a clergyman holding somebody's hand in public,' said Dora chattily. 'I don't know why, but it does ... After all a clergyman is a man and entitled to human feelings'.
>
> It was obvious to me now that she was in the kind of mood to disagree automatically with everything I said, for usually she maintained that clergymen didn't count as men and therefore couldn't be expected to have human feelings.

Similarly, in *A Few Green Leaves:*

> Tom, being the rector of the parish, hardly seemed in [Emma's] eyes to count as an eligible man.

In *Excellent Women*, old Mrs Beamish says:

> 'It will be quite like old times to have a priest in the house again.'
> 'So handy for you,' [Miss Prideaux] said.
> I wanted to laugh, for it sounded so odd the way Miss Prideaux put it, as if Father Ransome might be useful for chasing burglars, mending fuses or other manly jobs.

In *Jane and Prudence*, Nicholas is drying out his tobacco leaves all over the vicarage kitchen when Miss Doggett calls.

> To make matters worse, the vicar now emerged from behind a screen of leaves, his usual mild expression betraying that there was nothing at all extraordinary about the situation. He too was wearing a flowered apron which somehow took away from the dignity of his clerical collar, Miss Doggett felt.
> 'Well, there is no objection to the vicar hearing what I have to say,' said Miss Doggett.
> 'I feel I can almost count as another woman,' said Nicholas, perhaps rather too lightly.

Nicholas emasculated, both visually and verbally.

A character in *No Fond Return of Love* 'did not care for men, with their roughness and lack of daintiness, though the clergy were excepted, unless they smoked pipes.' And Ianthe Broome, whose father was a canon, 'did not like men very much, except for the clergy.'

In this matter, let Miss Doggett have the last word:

'A man can have his thoughts,' suggested Miss Morrow.

'Perhaps they do not care to be left alone with those,' said Jane. 'I often wonder when I leave Nicholas alone in his study.'

'But surely, Mrs Cleveland, a clergyman must be different. He would be thinking out a sermon or a letter to the Bishop.'

I shall conclude with *Some Tame Gazelle*. At the wedding of Harriet's beloved curate, there is cause for new hope:

'The third from the left,' whispered Harriet eagerly.

Belinda looked about her, rather puzzled. Then she saw what her sister meant, for in a corner she saw five curates, all young and pale and thin, with the exception of one, who was tall and muscular and a former Rugby Blue, as she afterwards learned.

The third from the left. How convenient of the curates to arrange themselves so that Belinda could so easily pick out Harriet's choice. He was dark and rather Italian-looking, paler and more hollow-cheeked than the others. ...

Belinda ... saw Harriet approaching with the new curate.

She smiled and shook hands with him, but before either of them could utter a suitable platitude, Harriet had burst in with the news that the young man was coming to supper with them on his first Sunday evening in the village, which would be in about a fortnight's time.

'He says he is fond of boiled chicken,' she added.

Now everything would indeed be as it had been before.

The Clerical Directory
from the novels of Barbara Pym

This directory is compiled by Father Gerard Irvine. The initials after each name represent the book(s), and the subsequent numbers the pages, in which that character appears. *'passim'* is used whenever there are constant references.

Abbreviations used: AFGL: *A Few Green Leaves;* AGOB: *A Glass of Blessings;* AAQ: *An Academic Question;* AUA: *An Unsuitable Attachment;* CTS: *Civil to Strangers;* CH: *Crampton Hodnet,* EW: *Excellent Women;* JAP: *Jane and Prudence;* LTA: *Less than Angels;* NFRL: *No Fond Return of Love;* QIA: *Quartet in Autumn;* STG: *Some Tame Gazelle;* TSDD: *The Sweet Dove Died.*

implies a Bishop; + departed

AINGER, Mark, Vicar, St Basil's, London NW (AUA passim; CTS 110)

AMERY, William. Curate to Hoccleve (STG)

AMIS, Curate at Central London church, (unidentified, but possibly St Albans Holborn) (LTA)

ANSTRUTHER, former Vicar St Basil's, London NW (AUA 65)

BODE, (Fr) Curate (later Vicar) St Luke, Notting Hill, address St Luke's Clergy House, London W12 (AGOB *passim*)

BOULTBEE, Curate to Canon Pritchard (JAP 235, 237)

BRANCHE, Basil. Curate to Canon Burdon. Vicar St Barbara-in-the-Precinct, London EC4 (AUA 149)

BRANDON, George William, Vicar SW13 diocese Southwark (LTA 77)

+BROOME, (Canon). Father to Ianthe Broome (AUA 18)

BURDON, Randolph, Vicar Mayfair. Uncle to Ianthe Broome (AUA 90)

+ BUSBY, Henry Bertram, 1st Vicar St Mary Pimlico (EW 155, 214)

CLEVELAND, Nicholas, Vicar: m. Jane Bold (JAP *passim*)

COFFIN, (Canon). Leader of church tour to Budapest (CTS 136)

DAGNALL, Tom, Rector diocese Oxford (AFGL *passim*)

DONNE, Edgar Bernard Amberley, Curate to Hoccleve; grandson of a Bishop, later College Chaplain (Oxford): m. Olivia Berridge (STG *passim*)

FORBES, Neville Arthur Brandon, B.A. (Lond.) 1937; Kelham Theol. Col. 1938; Curate West Hampstead 1940; Chaplain R.N.; St Ivel NW diocese London (NFRL *passim*)

GAYTHORNE, (Fr). St Jude, W.Kensington, diocese London (NFRL 102-3)

GELLIBRAND, ('Fr. G') Vicar, diocese Southwark (QIA *passim*). Brother to Dr Gellibrand (AFGL 2)

GLOVER, (Canon), former Curate to Hoccleve (STG)

+ GRAY, m. Allegra Gray (EW)

GREATOREX, Curate St Mary Pimlico, *address*: Grantchester Square SWI (EW 66)

GRIFFIN, Chaplain in Italy (EW)

\# GROTE, Theodore, vid. sub. MBAWAWA

\+ GRUNDY, DD. Chaplain of the Riviera dio Gibraltar (AFGL)

HARVEY, Canon, former Curate to Archdeacon Hoccleve (STG 64)

HOCCLEVE, Henry (Archdeacon), m. AGATHA, daughter of a Bishop (STG *passim*)

JAMES, Theodore, priest friend of Stephen Latimer (CH 157)

KENDRICK, (Canon) Rector St Ermin's, Belgravia SWI (STG)

LANGBAINE, William, member of Church tour to Budapest (CTS 140)

+LATHBURY, father Mildred Lathbury (EW)

LATIMER. Stephen. Curate St Botolph Oxford, *address*: Leamington Lodge, Banbury Rd. Oxford (CH *passim*)

\+ LAW, James Edward Ferguson, Vicar SW13 (LTA 196)

LESTER, Vicar of a country parish; formerly in London W12 (AGOB 49, 89, 188)

LEWIS, (evangelical) Vicar of a 'seaside town' (EW23)

LOMAX, (Fr.) Vicar of St Stephen's (JP 211)

LYDELL, David. m. Beth Doughty (QIA 39)

MALORY, Julian. Vicar St Mary Pimlico SW1 (EW *passim*, GOB 123, AUA 111)

\# MBAWAWA, Bishop of, Theodore GROTE, formerly Curate to Archdeacon Hoccleve. m. Connie Aspinall (STG 171ff)

+MOBERLY, Edgar Chaplain at Helsingfors; *address*: The Close, 12 Kalevatan, Heisingfors (CTS 180)

\# NYBONGALAND, Bishop of. Cousin to Miss Moberley (CTS 177)

\+ \# OGG, Bishop (CTS 180)

OKE, Canon, Vicar of 'home parish' of Mr Bompas (CH 5)

\# OPOBO and CALABAR, Oliver Bishop of (STG 148)

PALADIN, Edmund, M.A. (Oxon) (1st Theology) Curate Upton Callow (CTS 32ff)

PALFREY, Thomas, Canon m. 'kinswornan' of Bishop Ogg (CTS 180, 219-20)

PRITCHARD, Canon. Predecessor to Nicholas Cleveland (JAP *passim*)

RANSOME, Marius Lovejoy, M.A. (Oxon), Ely; Curate St Mark Wapping, St Gabriel N. Kensington; St Luke/Notting Hill, W 11; Vicar a suburban parish (AGOB *passim*)

RERESBY-HAMILTON, Vicar St Anselrn's E 1. (AGOB)

SAINSBURY. Edwin, Vicar St Lawrence. Holland Park W 11 (AGOB 167)

SMITH (Fr) locum at St Ivels NW (NFRL. (248)

\+ SPOFFORD. Ernest Hugh la Motte, former Vicar SW 13 (LTA)

STILLINGFLEET, (Revd) ex-missionary from Africa; *address*: Normanshurst Nursing Home (AAQ *passim*)

\+ STONEBIRD, Vicar Diocese London (LTA)

SUMMERHAYES, Vicar of Central London church (unidentified, but possibly St Alban's Holborn) (LTA 196)

TAVISCOMBE, (Devon) Vicar of (NFRL 183)

TEEP, (Canon), Uncle to Willie Teep (CH 213)

THAMES, Oswald, Vicar St Luke, Notting Hill. London W *address*: Villa La Cererentola. Siena. Italy (AGOB *passim*, AUA 93; FGL 87; QIA 203)

+ TOTTLE, (Canon), friend of Miss Morrow (CH 117)
TRENDY Tony, nickname for neighbourng Vicar to Fr. Gellibrand (QIA 133)
TULLIVER, Laurence Folkes Vicar SW 13 (LTA 80, NFRL 154)
WARDELL, Benjamin, Vicar of St Botolph, Oxford (CH *passim*)
WILMOT. Rockingham, Rector Upton Callow (Salop) (CTS 12)

Religious orders

(C of E)
St Basil's, London NW2 (TSDD 110)
St Hildelith, London SW (AGOB 125)

(RC) Order of St Anthony:
Fr.Egidio GEMINI (LTA *passim*)
Fr. SERPENTELLI (LTA 170)

(RC) secular
Frs. O'HALLORAN and KINSELLA (LTA 192)
Fr. BOGART St Aloysius, Pimlico (EW 22: 60)

Ex-Anglican priest
Mr. Towers (AGOB 74)
Adam Prince (AFGL 25)

Other denominations
BENGER, Fr. Francis (NFRL 143)
OLATUNDE, Jacob, Minister of charismatic Black Church (QIA 61)

Lay assistants
Sister BLATT (EW *passim*)
Sister DEW (AUA *passim*), later Warden of Normanshurst Nursing Home (TSDD)
FELL, Miss (CMS Missionary from Uganda NFRL 175)

Identifications
St Ermin's, Belgravia: St. Peter's, Eaton Square
St Mary's, Pimlico: St. Gabriel, Warwick Square
St Luke's, Notting Hill: All Saints' Notting Hill
Central London Church visited by Catherine Oliphant: St Alban's Holborn
Tom Dagnall's Parish in West Oxfordshire: presumably Finstock

Social class and the clergy

Tim Burnett

Social class is one of the principal motors of Pym's fiction and certainly one of the principal sources of her humour. The attitudes of the upper-middle class (which is what so many of Pym's characters, with their private incomes and secure lives, so clearly belong to) in her time, tended to be inflexible and freely expressed. Social sensitivity, let alone political correctness, lay a long way ahead. Their prejudices were unthinking and often therefore curiously without malice. "He's not a bad chap, for a Jew-boy" would be said with warmth rather than scorn. Apart from Jewish people, the other three unacceptables were Blacks, Gays and Roman Catholics. The attitude to Black people was more paternalistic and colonial than domestic, since there were virtually no Black people in Britain. Indeed, during World War II British people were intrigued by, and welcoming of, Black American soldiers – and were shocked by segregation in the US Army. Prejudice against Roman Catholics was as strong if not stronger than that against the other groups. They were seen as not quite English; indeed the majority of English Catholics were either from Ireland or from Continental Europe, and their practices were mysterious and felt to be somehow sinister. My father declared that he would rather that I married a black girl than a Roman Catholic. I ought to have defied him by seeking out an African Catholic girl, perhaps an Ibo, and thus covered both bases.

Prejudice on the ground of religion was not confined to Roman Catholics. The passage from *Jane and Prudence* where Fabian Driver walks down the village High Street from the pub to his house sums it up beautifully:

> He walked slowly down the main street, past the collection of old and new buildings that lined it. The Parish Church and the vicarage were at the other end of the village. Here he came to the large Methodist Chapel, but of course one couldn't go there; none of the people one knew went to chapel, unless out of a kind of amused curiosity. Even if truth were to be found there. A little further on, though, as was fitting, on the opposite side of the road, was the little tin hut which served as a place of worship for the Roman Catholics. Fabian knew Father Kinsella, a good-looking Irishman, who often came into the bar of the Golden Lion for a drink. He had even thought of going to his church once or twice, but somehow it had never come to anything. The makeshift character of the building, the certain discomfort that he would find within, the plaster images in execrable taste, the simplicity of Father Kinsella's sermons intended only for a congregation of Irish labourers and servant-girls – all these kept him away. The glamour of Rome was obviously not there.

> There remained only the Church of England, and here there was at least a choice between the Parish Church and Father Lomax's church - in the next village, but still within reasonable distance. It was natural to Fabian's temperament to prefer a High Church service, incense and good music, vestments and processions, but Father Lomax discouraged idle sightseers and expected his congregation to accept the less comfortable parts of the Faith – going to

Confession, and getting up to sing Mass at half-past six on a winter morning. So there was really nothing for it but to go to the Parish Church, where, even if the service was less exotic, the yoke was easier.

Non-conformity was clearly out. (I always find it rather sad that the grand old Quaker families who did so much to build British industry and philanthropy have now almost all become Church of England – but then I suppose something similar happens in the US when families as they become richer and grander become Episcopalian). Roman Catholics were out unless they were part of the small inbred group of Old Catholic Families, recusants who had never embraced the Reformation despite all that fines and civil disabilities could do to persuade them. And, *pace* Barbara Pym, who when she went to live in Pimlico became intrigued by Anglo-Catholicism with its smells and bells, "spikey" Anglicanism was out too. I do not recall ever having set foot in an Anglo-Catholic church until I went up to Cambridge and took to frequenting Little St Mary's, where the incense was so thick that one could scarcely see across the nave. I have heard people of my parents' generation say that the smell of incense made them feel physically unwell. As Belinda in *Some Tame Gazelle* remarks anxiously about Father Plowman:

'But Harriet, he *is* rather high. He wears a biretta and has incense in the church. It's all so - well – Romish.' Broad-minded as she was, Belinda was unable to keep a note of horror out of her voice.'

The reaction of Dulcie Mainwaring when she stepped into the porch of St Ivel's Church sums up the general attitude:

Another notice-board gave the services for the week typed on a printed form with little crosses at the corners. 'Confessions – Saturday 6.45', she read with a shudder. So it was High Church and Aylwin Forbes's brother might very well be unmarried.

In London at least Anglo-Catholic churches tended to be in working-class districts: Pimlico, Pentonville, or Holborn, for example. There they brought colour and drama into the lives of the toiling masses. I sometimes feel that Barbara Pym's High Church leanings mean that she gives that branch of the Church of England rather more prominence in her novels than it really would have had in middle-class lives at the time. Most people would have regarded taking Communion every Sunday with horror; once a month would have been quite enough, or preferably three times a year. Mattins and a good sermon were what most church-goers required.

Reflecting on Pym's churchmen and churchgoers reminds us that many of them are financially secure – even well-off. Archdeacon Hoccleve in *Some Tame Gazelle* clearly wants for nothing. He has a vicarage where several guests may stay in comfort at one time, a gardener to tend the spacious grounds (a gardener who cannot bear him because he wants hahas and yew trees and other such upper class adornments), and indoor servants too. His wife's foreign travel – at a time when it was relatively much more expensive than it is today – appears not to be limited by financial considerations. The Archdeacon may not have felt well off –

who among us ever does? – and he may have wished Lady Clara Boulding would attend his church rather than that of Father Plowman where she was wont to put five or ten pounds into the collection bag on Easter Sunday, the day when the collection traditionally is for the benefit of the incumbent, but he was immensely much better off than his equivalent would be today. For one thing, the spacious rectories and vicarages have mostly been sold off by the Church, to be replaced by mean and cramped little boxes. For another thing, the Church of England's revenues in those days were not pooled so that the clergy might be paid a uniform stipend. Each parish supported its own incumbent, and some livings were extremely well-endowed with glebe land and other investments. Others were not, and one wonders whether Father Plowman, as he sat wondering whether there would be refreshments at the Archdeacon's garden-party, had one of these less than fat livings.

With wealth and a dignified habitation came status, and a well endowed parson was the equal of the gentry – indeed, often came from a gentry family. The system of advowsons, whereby the Lord of the Manor often had the gift of the Living to bestow where he saw fit, meant that he could look after worthy but less well-to-do relations. Sometimes, indeed, the owner of a living bestowed it on himself. George Nathaniel Curzon, afterwards First (and last) Marquis Curzon of Kedleston, who as an Oxford undergraduate was described in rhyme as a most superior person, whose hair was long and dark and sleek, and who dined at Blenheim twice a week, claimed that he was middle-class because his father was a parson. Lord Scarsdale, the father in question, being in Holy Orders, had appointed himself to his own Living, the parish church being, conveniently enough, immediately behind his stately Adam pile, Kedleston Hall.

Clergy wives:
Roman matrons and Christian martyrs

Triona Adams

In the novels of Barbara Pym we can locate two essential poles to which her clergymen's lives gravitate to differing degrees. The Roman idea (perhaps I should emphasise here that I use *Roman* in the sense of Ancient Rome and not in the sense of Roman Catholic!) may be seen to be pushing the point, but the more we attempt to separate and categorise the women, excellent or not, in the final analysis, we come to a deeper distinction that that between Allegra Gray's silver fox fur and Jane Cleveland's baggy tweeds. I do not think that it is pushing this topic too far to say that the fundamental difference is religious belief; the varying degrees to which God and spirituality are actually part of the consciousness of the vicar's wife. Naturally, and indeed primarily, much humour is afforded by the well-observed narration of these women's lives, all, as we are so often told, in the rarefied atmosphere of an Austen novel. In Pym we certainly find Augustan wit but it exists against a backdrop of influence from the Victorian romantic novel: Victorian courtship is constantly foregrounded and then debunked. The figure of the matron is identified by her powerful personality and her power over others, especially her husband. The 'martyr' image comes from the mouth of Henry Hoccleve – this is his term for church-going spinsters and disappointed women. Sometimes – in Pym if not in life – they marry clergy or reject their proposals, or some, notably Jane Cleveland, achieve martyrdom within marriage or, rather, have it thrust upon them. In the end, it is not exactly a pretty picture. There are too many arrogant clergy, too many unsuitable or unpleasant wives in what often seems to be a clear-sighted but pessimistic picture of Church of England personnel.

Evidently church life and church people are an essential and recognisable ingredient of Pym: pitch pine and crimson lake, hungry curates and flower arranging. Robert Liddell, mutual friend of Barbara and Henry Harvey, defined this shared interest as 'ecciesiology' 'which included a kindly (and I hope not irreverent) amusement at the vagaries of clergymen in all denominations.' It is surely partly this that begs comparisons with Austen and we have heard so many of these: 'Barbara Pym's sly comic novels always remind me of Jane Austen let loose in Cranford.' (Jilly Cooper) 'Pym has applied Jane Austen's method to contemporary life'. However, I was interested to read this in *The Sunday Times* from Rachel Billington, who has embarked on writing a sequel to *Emma* . She writes: 'I soon came to the conclusion that the themes that preoccupied this nicely brought up spinster daughter of a vicar were love (not excluding sex), marriage and money. Religion hardly figured at all. Morality was very important indeed, but morality in relation to other human beings – not God.' I think that Billington is misguided here, forgetting that faith is so firmly rooted in Austen: clergy – the defenders of the moral realm – being equal to the military – the defenders of the nation – as her most favoured professions. Both are integral to the security of her England. At any rate, the critics are not united in finding in Pym a sustained similarity to the Austen voice, namely Nicholas Shrimpton and Marilyn Butler, both currently of Oxford university. In the *London Review of Books* in 1982, Butler cites *Mansfield Park* as a useful comparison of difference: '... that most ecclesiastical of the Austen canon may criticise the way in which the church is sometimes served by individuals but does not question its local importance as the corner-stone of the village community nor doubt its national role. It is not nearly so obvious in a Pym novel what is holding England together.' We must recognise the validity of Butler's assessment of Austen, but surely it is precisely this that is akin to Pym. Pym has her own distinctive voice and part of its definition, part of our recognition of it, is certainly centred on her treatment of the church. This does reveal a disparity with Austen's view, a more sanitising perspective and, frequently, a more pessimistic one, one that might lead the reader on to consider what, if anything, is holding England or ourselves together. Piers points out, 'aren't we all colleagues in a sense, in the grim business of getting through life as best we can?'

This is not to say that an examination of vicar's wives in Pym evinces a study of Pym's attitude to the church or the woman's place within it, but we can safely assume that she intends us to evaluate the coin by looking at both sides.

So, let us turn to the wives themselves and what they do. The vicar's wife's work is never done and her duties must span, perhaps to an even greater extent than her husband's, the full gamut of trivialities and great events of human life.

Rodney Forsyth in *A Glass of Blessings* comments, in regard to the notice on Father Thames' front door bell, 'I should have thought all clergy business must be urgent ... they are concerned with the fundamental things after all, birth, marriage, death, sin – though I suppose they are also besieged by idle women wanting to know about jumble and things like that.' Already women, albeit not clergy wives, are relegated to non-urgent business. Mildred Lathbury, as a vicar's daughter, appears to have all the necessary qualifications, including the ability to make the right noises at the right time.

> Platitudes flowed from me, perhaps with my parochial experience I know myself capable of dealing with most of the stock situations or even the great moments of life – birth, marriage, death, the successful jumble sale, the garden fete spoilt by bad weather . . . ."Mildred is such a help to her father," people used to say after mother died.

It reminds us of the Bishop of Mbawawa's song that can be adapted to any great occasion in life or death. Whilst Pym never puts the job description quite so baldly as this, it is useful to turn to Alan Bennett's monologue *A Bed Among the Lentils,* where vicar's wife, Susan, contemplates her life and duties.

> One of the unsolved mysteries of life, or the unsolved mysteries of my life, is why the vicar's wife is expected to go to church at all. A barrister's wife doesn't have to go to court, an actor's wife isn't at every performance, so why have I always got to be on parade? Not to mention the larger question of whether one

believes in God in the first place. It's assumed that being the vicar's wife, one does, but the question has never actually come up, not with Geoffrey anyway. I can understand why, of course. To look at me, the hair, the flat chest, the wan smile, you'd think I was just cut out for God. And maybe I am, I'd just like to have been asked, that's all. Not that it matters of course. So long as you can run a tight jumble sale you can believe in what you like.

Susan is a martyr, and probably a Christian one, as her struggle with faith indicates a greater awareness of its importance than that of her strongly career-minded husband. The further we explore the clergyman's wife the more we must come to realise that the issue of belief and the idea that the wife's 'job' and inter-personal skills might sometimes leave the fundamental ideas of faith behind.

So we turn to *Some Tame Gazelle,* where the archetypal matron Agatha Hoccleve presides over the triangle that includes Henry and Belinda Bede. Before we meet Agatha, we realise that she is where Belinda wants to be and the reader naturally feels disposed to regard her as something of a villain or worse, a *well-dressed* villain.

She is not inappropriately glamorous, but Mrs Prior grudgingly admits that Agatha's clothes are from 'the best houses' – a phrase that continues to rankle with Belinda through the novel.

'It isn't right,' thought Belinda indignantly, 'for a clergyman's wife to get her clothes from the best houses. She ought to be a comfortable, shabby sort of person, in an old tweed coat and skirt or sagging stockinette jumper suit. Her hats should be shapeless and of no particular style and colour. Like my old gardening hat.'

In fact, Belinda seems to be describing Jane Cleveland. We soon see Agatha in her managerial glory at the vicarage garden party – there certainly seems to be a slightly Roman reference in Pym's image of Agatha triumphant in the skirmish over Lady Boulting's marrows.

Belinda felt herself hurrying away, routed was perhaps the word, Agatha triumphant. It was a pity they sometimes had these little skirmishes, especially when Agatha was so often triumphant. All over two marrows, even if they *were* the finest on the stall.

Of course, we know that Archdeacon Hoccleve is the object of Belinda's true love but he is scarcely flawless in his self-dramatisation. It takes Belinda's affection to show him in a kindly light and even here the reader cannot be wholly convinced:

Only Belinda was unoccupied, but she was quite happy in the knowledge that the party really had been quite successful. Of course, if the Archdeacon had not been asleep, she could have had some conversation with him, but it was nice to know that he felt really at home.

Dr Pavell had looked forward to Belinda's captivating Henry but while he dislikes Agatha, 'he could not help admiring her skill,' when, by her powers, her husband was raised to Archdeacon. Belinda's devotion is all very well but it wouldn't have made Henry an Archdeacon and then he really would have a burden to complain of. He *needs* an Agatha figure, as is demonstrated when, in her absence, even Belinda takes on something of a hectoring tone.

"Isn't that seat rather damp?" inquired Belinda sharply. "We had some very heavy rain during the night and you know how easily you catch cold." She felt that as Agatha was so many miles away she was justified in adopting this almost wifely tone towards him. He looked up irritably. Belinda had spoilt the romance of his environment. It was just the kind of remark Agatha would make and, now that he came to think of it, he supposed the seat *was* rather damp.

Perhaps Belinda, though never as powerful as Agatha, might well have become a little more harassed and hectoring if she had married Henry, and just as much in need of a holiday in Karlsbad. In any case, although Belinda sometimes thinks Agatha would do better to humour him more, she *can* manage him admirably.

'Yes, I think Mr Donne was remembering the Latin, *colere*, which has the double meaning of dig and worship, as in cult and agriculture,' said Agatha helpfully. 'You explained it so well in your sermon about the spiritual meaning of harvest time,' Agatha added, turning to her husband. 'It would be nice to hear that again.' The Archdeacon looked pleased. Belinda was silent with admiration. What a splendid wife Agatha was! She could never have dealt with him half so cleverly herself, she thought humbly.

Henry enjoys feeling he's married the wrong woman, but really only sees Belinda as a potentially more lavish housekeeper and mute admiring audience.

Agatha has her follower in the story in the shape of Olivia Berridge. In her match with curate Edgar Donne neither love nor faith come into it. Evidently, Edgar would never have got around to proposing to Olivia, so Agatha shows us how it is done.

'It is not at all unusual. Men are understandably shy about offering what seems to them very little and when a woman realises this she is perfectly justified in helping him on a bit, as it were.' At this moment, an idea came into Belinda's head. At first it seemed fantastic, then quite likely and finally almost a certainty. Agatha had proposed to Henry. Why had this never occurred to her before? And now that it had, what was the use of it?

The probability is that Henry would never have got round to asking Belinda and she could never have dreamed of asking him.

Olivia Berridge is certainly not as stylish as Agatha, but is a strident matron in ill-fitting tweeds with long, narrow English women's feet in sensible shoes and good, heavy silk stockings. Her engagement speech proclaims her as a good match for Edgar but, rather too prosaic as she is, Pym allows Harriet to bring her down a little:

There was comfort in her words, as if she were protecting Mr Donne in a sensible tweed coat or even woollen underwear. It was obvious that she could take care of him, not letting him cast a clout too soon. She would probably help with his sermons too, and embellish them with quotations rather rarer than her husband, with his third class in theology, could be expected to know. A helpmeet indeed. "Rather toothy when she smiles, isn't she?" whispered Harriet.

This is not the only prospective marriage in the story. We cannot forget the rakish Don Juan figure of Theodore Grote, Bishop Mbawawa, yellowed and toothy. His proposal is truly awful in its comedy as he assures Belinda that she is 'quite equal to being the wife of a bishop,' not to mention remarking that he requires neither love nor a woman 'fair to outward view.' He is not unlike *Crampton Hodnet*'s Stephen Latimer, when he proposes to Jessie Morrow with the actual thought that 'he might do worse than marry Jessie Morrow.' Theo Grote admits that in his youth he used the celibacy of the clergy as a kind of protection, but we may begin to wonder if it afforded the women a greater safeguard. Certainly it seems that the men have everything to gain. We must pity Connie Aspinall who succumbs to Grote in the Army and Navy Store. What seems even more bizarre in Agatha's rekindled flame for Bishop Mbawawa. The Archdeacon envies the curate and Father Plowman the attention, jelly and socks lavished upon them by the parish martyrs because Agatha is too busy with real parochial work to indulge him, but she does make ill-fitting socks for Theo Grote, a humanising factor in Belinda's view of her rival. Both women love really rather hopelessly flawed and self-centred men, and Agatha's affection for Grote must be compared with Belinda's for Henry – neither are love's young dream, but the women see only their first loves. In the end, however, Agatha remains in control, but while she is still resplendent, she is no longer the cold image of 'Agatha triumphant' as we, and Belinda, have shared her secret for a little, yet she remains a figure of respect.

> Now Belinda knew there could never be anything pathetic about Agatha. Poised and well-dressed, used to drinking champagne, the daughter of a bishop – wife of an Archdeacon – that was Agatha Hoccleve.

Whilst we do not warm to Agatha, but come to respect and even sympathise with her, Allegra Gray in *Excellent Women* remains, as Sister Blatt would have it, 'a real viper' in silver fox fur. She is the worst kind of Matron and certainly seems to have little respect or time for any Christian values, other than clergymen. She is sheltered by her clergy widow status which is her cover, as Mildred comments: 'It seemed like a magic formula. So she's beautiful as well as good. That sounds almost *too* good to be true.' Which, of course, it is. As Mildred observes:

> Mrs Gray was good-looking and nicely dressed, rather *too* nicely dressed for a clergyman's widow, I felt, remembering many such who I had met before. Her quiet manner suggested self-sufficiency rather than shyness and there was something secret about her smile, as if she saw and thought more than she would reveal.

She is truly dreadful in sitting back, stroking her hair while she lets Winifred and even Mildred run up her curtains for her. She is a man's woman and at times like this, with only a female audience, does not bother with the whole act for women, who are actually more perceptive than she realises, and in fiction at least, this is her downfall. Even Winifred begins to sense disaster as things start to bubble under at that great Anglican institution – church flower arranging. The incident occurs as Allegra Gray takes charge and designates Lady Farmer's lilies to a jar on the floor when they traditionally go on the altar. Later, when Winifred flees to Mildred's protection, this snub comes out in all its glory. Poor Mildred has heard it all before.

> I suddenly felt very tired and thought how all over England, and perhaps indeed, anywhere where there was a church and a group of workers, these little frictions were going on. Somebody else decorating the pulpit when another had always done it, somebody's gift of flowers being relegated to an obscure window, somebody's cleaning of the brasses being criticised when she had been doing them for over thirty years ... and now Lady Farmer's lilies on the floor and peonies on the altar – an unheard of thing! But here, of course, there was more to it.

Allegra over-estimates her powers over Julian Malory, however, and Mrs Morris triumphantly reports the grand finale as heard by Mrs Jubb. Apparently, Mrs Gray renounced clergymen for good.

> 'She said something about them not knowing how to treat a woman and no wonder.' Mrs Morris paused, a little puzzled. 'I don't know what it was no wonder about, Mrs Jubb didn't say'

– which reminds us of Miss Doggett's dark observation that 'men only want one thing' but she appears unable to remember quite what it is.

As to Mildred, it is not unnatural that Rocky should keep referring to Julian as her property and she is indeed an ideal clergy wife, not only a rational organiser of unusually clear-sighted perception, but a vicar's daughter and a conscientious Christian. In a sense, of course, she is a martyr and Helena Napier is quick to emphasise this as a failure. "Of course, you've never been married,' she said, putting me in my place among the rows of excellent women." If Mildred is the ready-made vicar's wife, the prospect of Julian Malory, with incumbent sister, is not an attractive one, her readers would agree, and we must appreciate Mildred's frustration when the majority of the parish including Allegra and indeed, Julian, *persist* in regarding her as a slighted woman. In this light, Julian's approach to proposing to Mildred is all the more mundane as it builds on his assumption, which we know to be far off the mark, that Mildred is, and has been for all of three years, just waiting for him to make the first move. The way Pym undercuts his dialogue with the everydayness of the electric fire is wonderful; not here the windswept moors and blazing hearth, but slight drizzle on the wrong side of Belgravia.

> 'I know the kind of person I should like to marry,' he went on, 'and I thought I had found her. But perhaps I looked too far and there might have been somebody nearer at hand.' I stared into the electric fire and wished it had been a coal one, though the functional glowing bar was probably more suitable for this kind of occasion.

Mildred's subsequent commitment to Everard Bone, albeit primarily secretarial, does not seem substantially more heartfelt: we are comforted that Everard is far better looking and it is one in the eye for Helena Napier and the rest of the cast – but is proof-reading superior to the duties of a vicar's wife? In fact, is anthropology so very different from the Church of England Mildred describes? Both anthropologists and clergy deal with the major events in the life of man, despite the fact that Mildred is initially surprised to see Everard at St Ermin's, presuming anthropologists to be unbelievers. It seems that Mildred ends up a vicar's wife type after all, and it would be easy to take the novel's streak of gloom further to discuss whether Mildred's rejection of, literally, a church wedding for an alliance with a science that may be seen to question God or Christianity but has a deeper significance than illustrating the charm of Everard's profile. There is a certain amount of irony in the final line that implies that she has not so much evaded as doubled her trouble:

> Another picture came into my mind. Julian Malory, standing by the electric fire wearing his speckled mackintosh, holding a couple of ping-pong bats and quoting a not very appropriate bit of Keats. He might need to be protected from the women who were going to live in his house. So, what with my duty there, and the work I was going to do for Everard, it seemed as if I might be going to have what Helena called 'a full life' after all.'

From one first-person narrator to another, we move to *A Glass of Blessings* and Wilmet Forsyth – or we might almost call her Wilmet Woodhouse in homage to Austen's *Emma,* as it is a novel about perception. To an extent, of course, all Pym books rely heavily upon the author's perception and powers of observation but also, as in *Excellent Women,* upon those of her heroine. Perception is more a theme in *A Glass of Blessings* where Wilmet is found, all to often, to be sadly lacking in a way that all our vicar's wives – Mary Beamish, Mildred Lathbury, Olivia Berridge, even Agatha and Allegra, and certainly Jane Cleveland – possess in full. Poor Wilmet – Father Thames is certainly erroneous in expecting or even hoping that she might be available for the position of housekeeper. As she pictures the three priests struggling to boil an egg, she reveals her own uncertainty as to the procedure.

Poor Wilmet, her central disillusionment is the meeting of Keith, evidently Piers' lover and knitwear model, but by the finish of the novel we are able to tot up a fair amount of activity that she has either misconstrued or failed to realise altogether; Rodney's near affair with Prudence Bates, even the romance between Sybil and Professor Root and certainly the romance between Marius Ransome and this novel's clergy wife triumphant, Mary Beamish.

Mary is introduced as a comic martyr – if a slightly pathetic figure – and the charm of the description lulls the reader into forgetting to what extent this is *Wilmet's* description:

> The kind of person who always made me feel particularly useless – she was so very much immersed in good works so splendid, everyone said. She was about my own age, but small and rather dowdily dressed, presumably because she had neither the wish nor the ability to make the most of herself. This particular morning, which seemed to me in my nastiness, to be the last straw, she had just

been to a blood donor session and had apparently come away sooner than she ought to have done.

Thus Mary is evoked as the perfect foil to Wilmet, of the same age but differing in every drab particular, the archetypal spinster martyr. The suspicion of Mary's having a crush on Marius is, similarly, shown by Wilmet as a fruitlessly hackneyed, dishearteningly predictable one.

Again, poor Wilmet Woodhouse, she fails to see that not only is Mary the ideal vicar's wife but, and she admittedly comes to learn this, that it is doubtful whether Marius even deserves her. It is evident that Marius had done most of the pursuing (presumably on his moped) but his initial valuation of Mary is the same as later in the story – to him she remains 'a very fine person.' When he first remarks upon this, it is with a thoughtful air so that we might almost suspect him of measuring her up as a vicar's wife. Wilmet is right to feel exasperated with him later on for repeating the remark: 'I felt impatient with him ... then I began to wonder whether it was the only thing he ever said about women, the only compliment he knew.' Whilst this is not quite the case, it does reveal that Marius had not moved on in his feelings for Mary, and although we do not hear his proposal, we may compare his egocentrism to Grote's and Latimer's. Wilmet wonders,

> as one so often does, whether, in spite of his being a clergyman, he was really good enough for Mary, but I could hardly ask that question in so many words. "You're very lucky," I said, "Mary is such a splendid person." "Yes, isn't she?" he agreed. "She'll be able to do so much for me."

This is a little different from Wilmet's initial reaction of surprise 'that such a good looking man as Marius Ransome should want to marry anyone so dim and mousy as Mary Beamish,' although she does see that steadying influence is just what is required. Even Wilmet, however, is impressed by the vision afforded us of things to come at the couple's new parish. Here, Mary comes into her own and with her old practicality finding a new assurance, she has her husband firmly, if dotingly in hand.

> I noticed Mary sitting quite near us, looking already like a vicar's wife in her grey coat and rather too sensible hat. I had decided the occasion called for something a little gay and was wearing an emerald green feather cap with my black suit.

It seems as if Wilmet deliberately sets herself and Mary in opposition again, but the green hat seems a little flippant, and this is not the easy assurance of the Wilmet who introduces us to Mary and who, despite feelings of inadequacy and recognition of Mary's good works, found it easy to feel superior. A particularly nice touch to Mary's new assurance is given when Marius wonders if his voice will last out for the entire 39 articles and:

> 'I think you can divide them between morning and evening, can't you?' said Mary practically. 'Ah, tea is coming, how lovely!'

Lastly we turn to Jane and Prudence. Jane Cleveland is not a spinster, but she is my ultimate Christian martyr among clergyman's wives in whom self-knowledge and acute perception add something of a tragic quality to her pathos, consistently aware of her own failings and her inability to achieve her ideal. Rather like Alan Bennet's vicar's wife, Susan, she is uncomfortable aware of her domestic shortcomings: in the absence of the cook her solution to dinner is to open a tin. She feebly admits her faults to all. Even serving Prudence sherry is fraught with implications. 'I've been such a failure as a clergyman's wife,' Jane lamented, 'but at least I don't drink; that's the only suitable thing about me.' When Prudence points out that alcoholism is scarcely an occupational hazard, Jane sighs, 'So even my not drinking isn't an advantage. I might as well take to it then.' It is a sad end to her young ambitions that had such Trollopian high standards. It seems that despite those glowing intentions, things quickly began to go wrong.

Jane is, nevertheless, a wonderful character, possessed of a unique, often comic, often moving purchase upon the world, and the reader must delight in her wealth of descriptions and perceptions. In Jane's mind, not only does the move to a new parish become intricately analogous with a trip to the cinema, but the image has a sense of metaphysical, spiritual darkness as well.

> 'We do not know what, if anything, has gone before or at the best we have a bald and garbled synopsis whispered to us by somebody on his way out: that's Canon Pritchard, of course.' 'Mother!' said Flora, a little desperately.

Whilst she is frequently described, in these flights of fancy, as 'losing consciousness of her audience' who are often bewildered and not infrequently annoyed, she keeps her readers firmly on her side.

Part of Jane's lack of success is her inability to humour petty faults and foibles and whilst the reader may see this as something of a virtue, it is not unnatural that it irks her fellow-characters. Her intervention in the vestry between Messrs Oliver and Mortlake is received coldly and the arch rivals almost band together against the well-meaning vicar's wife, but Jane is more than capable of shrugging off this rejection. The well meaning idea of holding the PCC meeting in the vicarage drawing room goes awry in a similar way as Oliver and Mortlake are spoiling for a fight. Beforehand, the assembled men compare Jane far from favourably with her predecessors. 'You never know, it might hold him back from promotion, said Mr Whiting. 'A man is often judged by his wife,' replies Mr Mortlake, echoing a sentiment that Jane has already heard expressed in connection with Fabian Driver and to which she had ruefully responded, 'Oh dear ..'. When the squabble over the parish magazine cover finally breaks, Jane rushes in rather ill-advisedly.

> Nicholas smiled unhappily. She would never learn when not to speak, he thought, with rather less affectionate tolerance than usual. Not for the first time he began to consider that there was after all something to be said for the celibacy of the clergy. Jane realised from Nicholas' laugh and the uncomfortable silence that followed that she ought not to have spoken. 'I wonder if a cup of tea would help us to see things in perspective,' she said quickly.

Sadly it is a sum of Jane's achievements that this must be the only occasion in a Pym novel, or indeed in English literary history, that tea is ill-timed. Yet hers was the right response really; an attempt to diffuse the atmosphere of a foolish dispute. There is better still to come, as Jane, never one able to indulge in wholly idle chit-chat, replies with comic acumen to Miss Grampton's wild (or faint hearted) praise of the refreshments. 'Well, it seemed a good idea,' said Jane. 'I always think that when I'm listening to some of these gloomy plays on the wireless, Ibsen and things like that, oh, if only somebody would think of making a cup of tea.'

Perhaps Nicholas is to be pitied. As has been implied, his wife's lacking certain skills must prove to be a disadvantage to him in his career. His usual attitude is one of indulgence for his wife, the 'great novel reader', but at times he wonders whether she is a little too much so for a vicar's wife. She chose to marry the man she loved. Back at college she remembers Nicholas, 'coming along the drive on his bicycle, little dreaming that he was to become a clergyman, though seeing him standing in the hall with his bicycle clips still on, perhaps she should have realised he was bound to be a curate one day' and the sacrifices since have been mostly hers.

Robert Emmett Long has observed that Jane's character is partly derived from that of Agnes Wardell, wife to the vicar of St Botolph's in *Crampton Hodnet*: vague to an astonishing degree, she comes to tea with her gardening shoes on. Yet surely Jane must also owe something to the original Margaret Cleveland, the frustrated female academic. Jane is a true scholar, maybe even a poet, and a rejected one. Her unique vision of the world, far beyond worrying about her slip showing, is lost upon those around her. Her one publication, a slim volume of essays on 17th-century poets, is now forgotten. In a half hearted attempt to return to her studies, she looks over her notes, although she can scarcely remember what her project was to have been – the papers are dusty and confused and the ink has turned an arid brown. She is reminiscent of George Eliot's Mr Casaubon in *Middlemarch*, who again is an almost tragic figure, not because he has no opportunity for his work but because it is worthless, 'like the waters which come and go where no man has need of them.' Then again, she may be compared to Dorothea Casaubon, stifled in her marriage to a pedant clergyman, a role that she cannot fulfil.

Anatole Broyard also attributes to Jane Cleveland a central role in Pym's 'clergymen', in 'Overflowing her Situation' (*New York Times Book Review* 1983):

Perhaps [Pym's] most brilliant achievement was the portrait of what might be called The Woman who Overflows the Situation. This woman, this archetype, this uneasy heroine of the ordinary life, is always reaching for a further reference ... Jane is perhaps the best example. Tall, thin, so badly dressed as to be satirical ... Jane is always saying the kind of thing that most of us repress as being too poetic or far-fetched ... Her ideas dwarf and embarrass the practical mind. Her standards, her incessant expectations, seem gawky against the resolutely low profile of the normal and everyday.

'Dwarf' is an admirable choice of verb, as Jane's poetic grasp on what really matters highlights the trivialities of the others. Not the least contributing factor to this attitude is Jane's consideration of God. She seems almost alone in the vicar's wives in her struggle to bring consciousness of God into the everyday and her own actions. Admittedly, this is sometimes shown to comic effect.

Jane tried very hard to realise the presence of God in the vicarage drawing room, but failed as usual, hearing through the silence only Mrs Glaze running water in the back kitchen to wash up the supper things.

While Jane's struggle must make us smile, we might also wonder how many of the assembled pious truly have God on their minds at all. In the light of the unfulfilled Christian scholar, the events of the PCC meeting have genuinely moving undertones. When Nicholas gently criticises her intervention, it is the last straw.

"Why should we always do what they want,' Jane burst out. 'Oh, if I had known it would be like this ...' She ran from the room and into the downstairs cloakroom where the sight of Nicholas' soap animals reminded her of her love for him and she might have wept had she not been past the age when one considers that weeping can do good or bring relief.

It is a very English sort of tragedy, in which the protagonist realises that her circumstances cannot be truly tragic, merely disappointing. She is also capable, however, of bringing consolation, as when she comforts Nicholas over Mr Oliver's move to Father Lomax:

'You can't help it if he quarrelled with Mr Mortlake and Mr Whiting and likes incense and all that sort of thing.'
'My poor Jane.' He put his arm around her shoulders and they gazed down together at the remains of their supper.
'What can any of us do with these people? We can only go blundering along in that state of life unto which it shall please God to call us,' said Jane. 'I was going to be such a splendid clergyman's wife when I married you, but somehow it hasn't turned out like *The Last Chronicles of Barsetshire.*'

I do not think that we would like Jane Cleveland in the Barsetshire mould of the strong clergy wife, such as Mrs Proudie, the 'woman behind' the bishop; a true Roman matron — she even dies standing up in the manner of the Emperor Tiberius, and is surely more worthy of comparison with Agatha Hoccieve if not quite Allegra Gray. Better to 'blunder along' to God's calling, not always seeing its rhyme or reason, but doing one's best and achieving, as Jane sometimes does, a certain radiance.

Ultimately, however, it is not a radiant picture of men's treatment of women, or of many marriages or, by association, if not of the church as an institution, then of the foibles of its local realities. If Agatha Hoccleve thrives in its atmosphere, the ideal matron, and Jane Cleveland's poetic sensibilities render her one of the church's domestic martyrs, we cannot say that the vision is an entirely happy one. When Mary Beamish's nice but dim, bluff brother describes Mary's testing her vocation at the convent in terms of a ploy to win Marius over, Wilmet is swift to contradict him.

'I'd never have thought her capable of such cunning. It only shows we should never underestimate women, doesn't it?'

'Men should never do that', I agreed. 'But of course, that wasn't the reason why Mary went into the convent.'

In overestimating her cunning, Mary's brother underestimates her true worth. Too often in the Pym novels, men underestimating women. Julian underestimates Allegra Gray's intentions, and Nicholas Cleveland underestimates his wife's suffering. In the clergy, these misapprehensions seem all the more frequent and incongruous, as we expect something extra from those of the spirituality. The wives possess the clear-sighted self-knowledge and, in cases like Jane Cleveland's, we almost wish for her sake that she did not: as George Eliot has it:

> If we had a keen vision and feeling of all ordinary human life, it would be like hearing the grass grow and the squirrel's heart beat and we should die of that roar that lies on the other side of silence.

Seeking Barbara Pym: A Pilgrimage

Father Gabriel Myers, OSB

Ask, and it shall be given unto you;
Seek, and ye shall find;
Knock, and it shall be opened unto you. (Matthew 7:7)

"It shall be given unto you."

Barbara's novels became deliberate choices for my bedside table several years after I entered the monastery. In the early 1980s I had read and enjoyed them at the recommendation of a clergy friend – an Anglo-Catholic friend, need I say! But it was only after I had left the Protestant ministry, gone over to Rome, entered the monastery, run away after one month, and re-entered the monastery ten months later, that I was beginning to realize, as Catherine Oliphant does on a sleepless night, "that we are strangers and pilgrims here and must endure the heart's banishment." Like her, I wanted to reach for a "nice book that would take me out of myself" *(Less Than Angels,* 138). When I reached for a novel by Barbara Pym, I found just that. If it did not bring permanent relief (as one of the products advertised on Miss Lord's television), it did bring little jokes to savor, a healing perspective, even comfort for the rough edges of communal living. One could almost say that such bedtime reading was one of "the various ways of mending a broken heart" (*No Fond Return of Love*, Chapter 1).

Although it was to be several years before I would find friends who knew the novels well enough to communicate in their terms, I suppose I began to practise the outlook when I was about 35. I was slightly past those days of wine and roses which are not long, past the first fervor of the new convert. And, indeed, there was in my community some unpleasantness which seemed impossible to resolve. In the words of Father Thames, now I was really in the soup and needed practical help more than prayers. And Barbara came to the rescue. I admit this without shame, for it is one of those rare instances when a man, even a clergyman, is guiltless when making someone an answer to prayer. It was surprising how often a characteristically Pym motif sprang to mind in the course of a week. I will limit myself here to naming just half a dozen of my favorites.

"Such richness!" Jane's repeated cry (with hands clasped in an affected manner and "much more in the same strain" (*Jane and Prudence,* 64) is, for me, the main key for unlocking the Pym jewel box. That a similar phrase about "material" was on Barbara's own lips when she entered the Michael Sobell hospice indicates that the perspective can be satisfying for a lifetime.

Embroidering a theme as Piers and Wilmet do about the furniture depository (GB, 70-75), as Catherine does (to Tom's annoyance) with the stone lions, or as Emma does (to Daphne's puzzlement) about a dog left in the flat all day. This is a great pleasure and cure for tedium, near at hand and costing nothing.

The Dominion of the Birds is my closest friend's favorite. "At least we can eat our enemies" (EW, 149) and how shocking it is that we occasionally wish to. Let me hasten to add that my friend is more kindhearted than I, more generous with Dulcie's practical sympathy for the disadvantaged, including "those two and their little dog against the world." (NFR, 76)

Spacing the treats (NFR, 44) as Dulcie does with outings for investigative research and Marcia does with doctor visits, is a whole philosophy of life. It calls to mind the biblical inheritance promised to the meek, and prevents one from becoming greedy like Old Mrs Beamish with her dripping chop!

Trivial pleasures Perhaps it is too obvious to mention the list inspired by Catherine's purchase of a real calf's foot? I too am fond of "little poems, especially sad ones" and "solitary walks" (LTA, 104). One also remembers Belinda's tears of joy ("her heart like a singing bird" in Miss Rossetti's phrase) when Miss Prior, finding the caterpillar in the cauliflower, confides that Agatha keeps a poor table.

A sense of the ridiculous, or the irony that Barbara missed in the novels she read for the Romantic Writers Association. I love to remember Edith Liversidge, smoking at the back of the church hall and looking for a good laugh. When the Bishop says, "Imagine yourself at an African wedding," I hear Edith growl, "I do not feel myself equal to that" (STG, 179). How often one wishes for the courage of such candor!

On the other hand, exercising the imagination is a pleasure when it is one's own choice. It is perhaps Barbara's chief legacy to her readers that she inspires us to do so. I have stretched my imagination and broadened my horizon in happy and beneficial ways over the years by reading the writers Barbara enjoyed – Philip Larkin, Christina Rossetti, the dear Earl of Rochester, so many of our greater English poets, all twelve volumes of Anthony Powell's Dance to the Music of Time, but not nearly all of Ivy Compton-Burnett, or of Henry James, whom "of course one has read, being so very much one's own kind of novelist". (SDD, 200). Closer to Barbara's own approach would be the prolific Victorian novelist Charlotte M. Yonge, in whose family chronicle The Daisy Chain Barbara delighted while grieving over Gordon Glover (VPE, 116) and again during the disappointing wilderness years (VPE, 260). I also read the autobiographical stories of Denton Welch, one of which appears, alongside Some Tame Gazelle, on Dulcie's bathroom shelf!

Finally, the shy and self-effacing author of my favorite bedside books inspired me to some boldness. It all started in the way Larkin's friendship with Barbara started, with fan letters to Barbara's sister and her biographer, which led to the occasional postcard, the exchange of Christmas cards and the sharing of Pym material from the stuff of daily life. There are unique pleasures to epistolary friendship, as Elizabeth Taylor shows in her story, The Letter Writers, so that one almost hesitates to close the gap of something that is so perfect from a distance.[1] But in the fullness of time, though less than the fourteen years before Barbara first met Larkin, there came an opportunity for some on-site visits and personal meetings. Thus it was that, as Barbara made "Denton Pilgrimages" to Greenwich and Middle Orchard, so too a friend and I made a "Barbara Pilgrimage" when we visited London in June 1998.[2]

Background Considerations

This essay strives to make its point chiefly by narrative. Indeed, it may emulate the Pym style too closely in its use of literary allusions, made to her novels and her favorite passages from the greater English poets. My efforts to imitate her approach, and in fact to tell a story, are intended to celebrate and keep her memory green. Nevertheless, it is well to consider the motivation for my pilgrimage. Why did I go? What did I hope to find? Did I not fear that the enchantment of Barbara's art would disappear when placed under the microscopic lens of immediate physical observation? Four responses seem to suggest themselves to these legitimate but difficult questions.

First, Barbara's own behavior in regard to her "oh darling Denton" inspired me. She delighted in "finding out" about people (*VPE* 10). Her solitary visit to Welch's Greenwich residence on a rainy day was scrupulously recorded and did not disappoint her despite the bleak detail: "Green plant (azalea?) in upper window. Tiny patch of rather bald grass in front with dustbins" (*VPE*, 198). A year later Barbara visited his more isolated residence in Kent (*VPE*, 198). An accompanying friend on this Denton Pilgrimage shared the "Denton Picnic," and served as driver down the "bumpy lane" (*A Lot To Ask*, 172). There is no indication that the pilgrims feared they were being intrusive.

Hazel Holt observes that Barbara

> might have been tracking down someone still alive, and, indeed, he was alive to her in a way that few authors ever were. ...She loved Denton for his acute, miniaturist observation and vibrant interest in everything he saw. ...Above all, he realized, as Barbara too had realized, the value of small comforts (of trivia) in an embattled life. He showed that this 'littleness' can build up into something moving and universal in the right hands. (*ALTA,* 173)

Through his writings Denton was for Barbara a kindred spirit and companion. In a similar way Barbara connects with me.

Second, Barbara's characters inspired me. Especially compelling as amateur detective is Dulcie Mainwaring of *No Fond Return of Love*, "the heroine most like Barbara herself" (*ALTA,* 182). While some critics look askance at the "snooping, spying, and tracking,"[3] Dulcie is rather perceptive about the pleasures, disappointments, and character flaws (if such they be) of someone who nurtures a relationship with a distant figure. She thus offers helpful commentary on the motivation for literary pilgrimage:

> 'I love finding out about people,' said Dulcie. 'I suppose it's a sort of compensation for the dreariness of everyday life....Perhaps other people's lives are a kind of refuge,' she suggested. 'One can enjoy the cosiness of them. ... [Or] find oneself looking at the horror or misery in them with detachment, and that in itself is horrifying.'(9)

> [T]his was really the kind of research Dulcie enjoyed most of all, investigation – some might have said *prying* – into the lives of other people. ... It was most satisfactory if the objects of her research were not too well-known... for it was rather dull just to be able to look up somebody in *Who's Who*, which gave so

many relevant details. *Crockford* was better because it left more to the imagination. (36). . . One goes on with one's research, avidly and without shame. Then suddenly a curious feeling of delicacy comes over one. One sees one's subjects-or perhaps victims is a better word-as being degraded by one's probings... (173)

In contrast to those who suggest patronizing explanations for an author's material-gathering techniques, I am impressed by Dulcie's candor. Surely, the consciousness of personal motivation, an awareness of the danger of violating personal privacy, and enthusiasm for imaginative exercise (*see*: saga-creation, *ALTA*, 175-76) are qualities worthy of respect. Perhaps in the balance she struck between curiosity and delicacy, Dulcie has something to say to scholars and biographers who may lack sufficient respect for the dignity of their subject's memory.

Third, Barbara *as a character* inspired me. Using an oddly postmodern technique of "breaking the fourth wall," Barbara permitted herself to appear in tiny walk-on cameo appearances at a number of points in her oeuvre. If this is authorial self-indulgence, I find it utterly charming. It is almost as if the reserved English lady lowers her guard ever so slightly, to reveal the exuberantly flirtatious undergraduate personality underneath. (During her university years, Barbara had indeed given this alter-ego free reign: in "scarlet satin blouse and tight black skirt, Sandra was, in fact, rather 'fast'" (*ALTA*, 28)). The reader, in a way, is thus encouraged to seek out the author. There are three especially striking instances of this beckoning finger.

Miss Bird at Jane Cleveland's literary society meeting. "After the first two or three [books] one must... consider one's public.... I have just finished my seventeenth – Miss Bird's readers know what to expect now and they will not be disappointed" (*JP*, 118-19).

The anonymous visitor at the dismal dinner in the guesthouse of bright Christian atmosphere. She was

ordinary-looking and unaccompanied, nobody took much notice of her. As it happened ... some of the [guests] had read and enjoyed her books, but it would never have occurred to them to connect her name with that of the author they admired (*NFR*, 179).

Penelope's difficult client at the publishers Toogood and Shelve (*UA*, 81). The publisher's rejection of *An Unsuitable Attachment* in 1963 was the beginning of many "wilderness years," during which Barbara continued to revise and submit the manuscripts. With amazing lightness of touch she is joking about this painful situation. Here she appears in the role she described to Philip Larkin as "indignant rejected middle-aged female author (a pretty formidable combination, don't you think?)" (*VPE*, 216).

For me, the traits of these three characters – zany self-confidence, quiet dignity, courage worn lightly – are compelling reasons to follow up with further investigation of the author.

Fourth, may I suggest without ponderous solemnity that the spiritual quality of the novels inspired me? Charles Burkhart calls attention to their optimism, bravery, and uniqueness in being "documents of faith and acceptance."[4] More surprising may be the praise of Joyce Carol Oates, whose vision and material are so different from those of Pym:[5]

> As a consequence of her gentle satirical humor, frequently directed against organised religion, ... it comes as something of a shock to realise she is, finally, a religious writer.

It is small wonder then that the diary scene of pilgrimage to the T.S. Eliot memorial at Finstock church, a happy moment shared by "two quiet people," rings a deeply felt chord in me.[6] Barbara felt that she and "two great poets came for a brief moment (as it were) together" when she and Larkin visited the Eliot memorial (*VPE*, (287). I am not the only reader who has wanted to join them there. Robert Liddell gently explains, "It is understandable that many readers have made pilgrimages to the place where she spent her last years, and some of the happiest times of her life."[7]

A final factor is my own Benedictine monastic tradition. Despite monasticism's emphasis on cloister and "staying put" by a vow of stability, the scriptural motif of "The Pilgrim's Progress" is deeply woven into the Rule of St Benedict in such images as "running the path" and "hastening toward our heavenly home."In fact, St Benedict's emphasis on the necessity of a novice being one who "truly *seeks* God" influenced the title of this essay.[8]

"Seeking"

There was something suitable about the lodgings for our "Barbara Pilgrimage," which were in Eaton Place – right around the corner from the elegant home of Julian Amery's mother – but in a decidedly *downstairs* apartment. The kindly retired Irish landlady made an excellent pot of tea (kept hot in a cat-shaped cosy); she loved talking of *home* in County Mayo though she had lived in London for some fifty years; she was fond of daintiness (the toilet's requisites were very pink and very fluffy); and one evening she entertained us with jigs and reels and melancholy airs on a miniature accordion! She thus was ripe, with a little polishing, to slip into a Barbara Pym novel.

On our first morning my friend and I walked from our lodgings into Pimlico, on the "wrong side" of Victoria, to visit St Gabriel's, Warwick Square, the prototype of the church in *Excellent Women*.[9] How astonished we were to discover that Barbara's actual address was right across the street from St Gabriel's noble spire! I had always imagined Mildred's much-loved view from further down the square, glimpsing the church in the distance. The house at 108 Cambridge Street (SW1), where Barbara and Hilary occupied a corner flat on the first floor, did not look at all shabby: the windows are large and the façade has a classical symmetry. Perhaps the Pym sisters did "raise the district's tone!" as Barbara once joked to Henry Harvey.

We were thrilled to perceive at the church that it was the morning for the cleaning rota. So a ring of the doorbell gained us a slightly hesitant admission: we were welcome to look around while they went on with their trivial round and common task. We walked through the vestry which Mildred described as gloomy and untidy, and into the large nave. The altar was beautifully vested. There were "Romish statues"– some wearing actual clothing – and, as in Italy, some artificial flowers at small shrines. We also noticed confessionals, but on a Wednesday morning there were no clergy lying in wait for the sensitive consciences of Anglo-Catholic ladies. Our hostess had been married at St Gabriel's in 1948. While she acknowledged some change and decay (the pipe organ needed repairs and the sandstone exterior was crumbling in a worrisome way), the fifty Sunday worshippers were served by three priests. "Two of them do it for love!" she announced with justifiable pride. We met one of the assistant priests outside, who also spoke with confidence of St Gabriel's ministry. "Our deanery is of one accord," he told us. "We do not suffer from the divisions and hesitations that our neighboring Roman brethren seem to be having." My friend and I, though both of Roman persuasion, went on our way encouraged. "We'll offer him up on Sunday," had been his parting words, the piety leavened by an almost chirpy delivery.

We then took the No. 36 bus, sitting on the upper level as excited tourists, to Queen's Park, NW 6. It must be only in comparison to the great London parks that Hazel Holt describes Queen's Park as a little oasis. There were wide manicured lawns, beautiful flower beds, little boys playing soccer near a banner saying "Sponsored by the Corporation of London." We saw old men on constitutionals, young mothers with strollers, and other inhabitants of the Larkin poem "Toads Revisited." None could answer our questions about the Church of St Lawrence the Martyr, formerly on Chevening Road, which had been declared redundant and closed despite the efforts of faithful members like the Pyms. So we finally decided that the modern flats on St Lawrence Close must have been the end of the Pyms' Sunday morning car chase tracking their intriguing neighbor Bear in his Hillman Husky (*ALTA*, 177-79).

We found net curtains on the downstairs window of 40 Brooksville Avenue, where the Pym sisters lived from 1961-1972. A large uncurtained bay window displayed a tree-like plant in the upstairs front room. So we wondered whether the present residents also used it as a sitting room in order to see the comings and goings, as Mabel and Rhoda did in *Less Than Angels*. Just below the upper window was a black medallion witnessing to the Pym association. I believe that the recognition of an official London blue plaque cannot be given until twenty years after the person's lifetime, so it was a joyful pleasure to find such a memorial. We had brought a camera to record our pilgrimage sites.[10] My friend tried to include me in a photograph showing both the gate and the door-number. This was not entirely successful. Then by crouching in the street (to use one of Barbara's favorite expressions) he hoped to include both me (smiling) and the medallion. The upper window remained a problem.

"I know!" he shouted with typical Italian exuberance. "Why don't you climb up on the gatepost, and then we'll have everything." A heated discussion followed in which I, of more retiring disposition, explained how unsuitable such typically rude and American tourist-behavior would be, how it would infringe upon the memory of Barbara's impeccable and fastidious manners. I was pulled up short by the volume of our American tourists' voices in this utterly silent street when the figure of a woman appeared in the upper window where the Pym sisters once sat. She was tall and friendly looking, apparently not cross with all our noise. She smiled and nodded briefly before disappearing. She was, in Mildred's words, "not pretty, but with quite a pleasant face" (E*W*, 137). I was not quick enough to notice whether her smile could be described as charmingly lopsided. But later I learned that the house was owned by two male colleagues, not a married couple. So who *was* that tall, pleasant-faced woman who nodded kindly to the American pilgrims? I should like to think that from the place where Tom Boilkin (named for his loud purr) drank some of the holy water when the vicar blessed the house on the Pyms' moving in in 1961, which the Pym sisters considered "a good omen" some of this supernatural power lingered some thirty-five years later, and there was still "virtue going out" in the form of this apparition, as if to bless our pilgrimage. [11] To us, it was a happy omen.

Two months later, after a ministerial internship at a Benedictine parish in Lancashire, I was again in London before returning to the USA. My spirits were a bit low because I had no travelling companion, and I was sad to bid England farewell. I even had some 'flu symptoms. Nevertheless, I took the tube to Hammersmith, questioning on the way a friendly Middle Eastern businessman about the way to Barnes, SW13, where the Pym sisters had a flat from 1949 to 1961.

Walking over the beautifully scroll-worked Hammersmith Bridge gave me the chance to think of Tom and Catherine walking – and arguing – *en route* to Sunday afternoon tea at the Swans. On the way there is a charming little park with a duck-pond. The front garden of 47 Nassau Road is entirely bricked over, but there are carefully tended vines and pot-plants. I could imagine Mrs Beltane, scented and braceleted, tending them with a watering can in the shape of a swan: an image for an unfinished poem. I thought of the young men, Bear and Squirrel, living a few doors up from the Pyms: those two and their little dog against the world.

With the help of several passers-by I found my way along the river to St. Michael's Church, which is in a quiet street and has a lovely garden. [12] The large gleaming blue signboard showed that parishioners get full Catholic privileges and at least one traditional Prayerbook Mass each week, but that the assistant priest and curate are women. To me, this seems a nicely balanced profile.

After my long walk I was fretful to find the church locked. I rang the vicarage doorbell and stammered out my plea to the young, handsome clergyman who answered. "I'm in a meeting right now," he answered, "but here is the key and a few postcards. It is a pity that we have never pursued the Pym connection, I suppose." At the back of the church were needlework kits for kneelers and a brand new set of *The New English Hymnal*, which I think (in Henry Harvey's phrase) "remarkably fine." "Dark churches are the best for praying in," as Robert Liddell shows in his novel of North Oxford. [13] I did not light a candle, as Barbara's friend

Skipper (Richard Roberts) once did with her in a little Roman church. But I think that it was a fitting place to end my Barbara Pilgrimage: in a dark church, alone, with a thankful heart.

"The Door Opened"

A more social and companionable experience was our visit to Finstock, the West Oxfordshire village where Barbara and Hilary made their home after their retirement in the early 1970s. Several days after the omen vouchsafed to us at Brooksville Avenue, my friend and I took a coach to Oxford, where, outside the Randolph Hotel, we boarded the Worth's bus service to Charlbury, alighting on a country road near Finstock. We had reserved the one suite at the Plough Inn, thatched and of honey-colored Cotswold stone, where we were welcomed by the proprietors. Nigel had the ebullient personality of Wilf Bason – next morning we caught him watering the flowers in bathrobe and scuffs, and wondered what Mrs Pope would say about growing slack! His brother Keith had the formal reserve of Mr Coleman, head of the servers at Wilmet's church. We were treated royally. The warning to be sure to draw our curtains seemed odd, but proved wise when a short afternoon "rest" was ended by what seemed an all-village fire-evacuation by way of the little path outside our door. Like Dulcie's at the learned conference, my alarm abated with the realization that the tramping footsteps were nothing more dangerous than enthusiasm for afternoon tea!

We visited the church, situated rather inconveniently on the main road outside the village. Originally a chapel of ease for the residents of the manor house, the parish which it serves is a recent, 19th-century creation, because the Wychwood Forest had been a royal property which theoretically had no human inhabitants. Thus there are no recumbent knights, or 18th-century wall tablets with weeping cherubs, in Holy Trinity Church, Finstock. But the interior has a few treasures: a window in honor of Queen Victoria's first Jubilee; a wood-framed copper plaque commemorating the secret baptism here in 1927 of T.S. Eliot ("Poet-Playwright-Critic"); another plaque to honor Barbara's writer-friend Gilbert Phelps, and an elegant Crucifixion in stained-glass above the proper English altar.[14] The chancel, with its choir and rood screen, was added to the original building in 1902 by a former rector ("in memory of my mother"), and may be slightly disproportionate to the modest dimensions of the country church.

On the wall towards the front, where Barbara usually sat, is a modest and tasteful grey granite oval plaque. The inscription reads, "Barbara Pym, Writer, Worshipped Here," with her dates. Near the chancel step is a mahogany lectern: neither bird nor brass, but well-polished wood can be very rewarding, as Miss Lee knew. Under its Bible is a tiny brass marker which says that Barbara "organized the Epistle readers" in her eight years at Finstock. The plaque and the lectern were given as memorials by her admirers in 1984. Since I had not contributed, I climbed (with permission) onto the organ bench and played two stanzas of George Herbert's hymn "King of glory, king of peace," which Barbara once described in her diary as "very English, like a damp overgrown churchyard" (*VPE*, 195).

Outside the church, in the shade of ancient yew trees, one is reminded of Gray's "Elegy" and of the Archdeacon quoting Young's *Night Thoughts*. There looms the fortress-like DuCros Family Vault (1899), where Tom and Dr G. meet unexpectedly, its severity begging for the floral ministrations of Terry Skate. Barbara's grave is not easy to find. The mossy headstone has settled at an angle, and the ground has returned to its natural state in accordance with her wish. At the gate is a path through the fields to the village, where one thinks of Barbara walking with Larkin, of his poem "Church Going," and the fine lines of John Donne:

When my grave is broke up againe
Some second ghest to entertaine ...

Difference of sex no more wee knew
Then our Guardian Angells doe.

But there is no time for brooding, for we have been invited to tea at Barn Cottage! The sofa pattern and the hearth are familiar from the photograph in the biography. There is a cat purring on a rug, and a "Whiskas" box among the kitchen canisters. The window over the kitchen sink, however, is a thousand times more cheerful than that in the Clevelands' vicarage. The sitting room is lined with books, prints, photographs: neat and cosy in the way I imagine Miss Prideaux's to be in *A Glass of Blessings*. There are so many impressions to take in that I feel a bit shy, and I am not tempted to Avice Shrubsole's sort of pushiness (asking for the loo as she heads up the stair) in *A Few Green Leaves*. The chief physical memories I carry away are a complete set of Elizabeth Taylor's novels, a handsome formal photograph of Barbara herself, and another intriguingly mysterious one of a handsome man in military uniform. Could this be a secret love of whom we know nothing? I learned, much later, that this was Henry Fiennes Crampton, the paternal grandfather unearthed by Hilary's genealogical research.

That evening the three of us dined, splendidly and memorably, in the fine restaurant at the Plough. The conversation was of music, church, and village life; there was happy laughter, and even a champagne glass broken as if for good luck. Under a gloriously star-strewn sky, undimmed by urban lighting, we said our good-byes at the door of Barn Cottage. I am sure that my eyes were shining with excitement, like Dulcie's when anticipating a trip to Taviscombe. Back in our suite, I read aloud the nicely printed booklet (which Hilary had given us) of Father William Jarvis's "Address on the Occasion of the Dedication of a Memorial Plaque and Lectern to Barbara Pym." It is a lovely and well-considered tribute to Barbara's art and to her Christian faith. I felt some of what Mildred must have felt, at the dedication of the window to Miss Ridout ("the Sturge we had called her"), about a teacher who had been kind, funny, and terribly influential in the formation of her own character (*EW*, 111).

At last I thought of the words of an obscure Victorian hymn by the famous anthologist and professor of poetry, Francis Turner Palgrave, who compiled *The Golden Treasury* and dedicated it to his friend, Lord Tennyson:

Where'er the gentle heart
Finds courage from above,
Where'er the heart forsook
Warms with the breath of love,
Where faith bids fear depart –
City of God, thou art.[15]

Gentleness, warmth, courage, even love (of gazelle or dove or poodle dog). Despite the vaguely Unitarian tinge of the lines, they serve well enough as a closing chorus for our visit to a West Oxfordshire village. I thought of some of the events that had brought me to this moment. Sometimes I had felt, like Alaric Lydgate, that "life was very terrible whatever sort of front we might put on it" (*LTA*, 57). At other times I had agreed with Catherine, who compared life to an old friend or tiresome elderly relative, "pushing, knocking, clinging" (*LTA*, 154). Occasionally the spirit of delight, immortalized by the poet, made its visitation. I did not feel so ambivalent about Barbara's novels. They had brought me to Pimlico, Queen's Park, Barnes, and Finstock. But, more important, they bring me fresh pleasure and new enchantment each time I open them. They are "just the ticket," as Norman would say, for what Dolly Arborfield (of *An Academic Question*) calls "Life's Journey."

Notes and References

1. Elizabeth Taylor, *The Blush and Other Stories* (Penguin, 1987).

2. Denton Welch (1915-48) was a talented art student of difficult temperament who found his true vocation as diarist and fiction writer after a crippling bicycle accident at the age of 20. He wrote persistently, despite great physical distress, until his early death.

3. Anne M. Wyatt Brown, *Barbara Pym: A Critical Biography* (University of Missouri Press, 1992), p. 97.

4. Charles Burkhart, *The Pleasure of Miss Pym* (University of Texas Press, 1987), p. 116.

5. Joyce Carol Oates, "Barbara Pym's Novelistic Genius," *The Life and Work of Barbara Pym*, ed. Dale Salwak (University of Iowa Press, 1987), p. 44.

6. Hazel Holt, "Philip Larkin and Barbara Pym: Two Quiet People," *Philip Larkin: The Man and His Work,* ed. Dale Salwak (Macmillan, 1989), p. 68.

7. Robert Liddell, *A Mind at Ease: Barbara Pym and Her Novels* (Peter Owen, 1989), p. 143.

8. Prologue, verse 49; Chapter 73, verse 8, and Chapter 58, verse 7, *The Rule of St. Benedict in English* (Liturgical Press, 1982).

9. My travelling companion was a fellow monk, Father Marc-Daniel Kirby, O.Cist., professor of liturgy at Holy Apostles Seminary, Cromwell, Connecticut.

10. This resulted in *A Barbara Pym Photograph Album*, with suitable captions, which has been enjoyed at meetings of the Pym Society. There is something here of Barbara's delight in preserving "relics".

11. Hazel Holt, *A Lot To Ask*. New York: E. P. Dutton, 1991, 185

12. A scholarly note of the sort that gave Barbara pleasure: the great Victorian hymn writer, John Ellerton, author of "The Day Thou Gavest," was Rector of Barnes, 1876-84. He was known for his "singular charm and strength of Christian character." His hymn texts, many of which are still in use today, reveal a gentle and truly sympathetic nature. I like to think that he would have enjoyed his parishioner's novels had he lived a century later.

13. Robert Liddell, *The Last Enchantments* (London: Peter Owen, 1991), 177-78.

14. Gilbert Phelps, "Fellow Writers in a Cotswold Village," *The Life and Work of Barbara Pym*, ed. Dale Salwak (University of Iowa Press, 1987), p. 34.

15. Hymn 259, *Hymns Ancient and Modern Revised*, (William Clowes, 1950), p. 347.

Miss Pym and the Victorian hymn

Fr Gabriel Myers, OSB

"I love Evensong," said Jane. "There's something sad and essentially English about it. ... We have the old hymns here. Ancient and Modern. Sun of my soul, thou Saviour dear ... the congregation love it and Nicholas wouldn't change it for the world" (*Jane and Prudence*, 174).

I share Jane Cleveland's preference for the sad, old-fashioned hymn, as I believe Barbara did herself. This enthusiasm was a genuine part of Barbara's devotional life, and yet she was able to use it to comic effect, as Mildred Lathbury shows when trapped into an impromptu date by Everard Bone. To break the awkwardness, Mildred (whose string bag holds a biography of Cardinal Newman) recalls a memory from school days:

> We were sometimes allowed to choose hymns, but Miss Ridout would never let us have 'Lead, Kindly Light' – she thought it was morbid and unsuitable for schoolgirls. Of course we loved it (*Excellent Women*, 142).

The hymn's uncertainty and anguish at being far from home are similar to another Pym favorite, "Dover Beach" by Matthew Arnold, used by Rupert to describe Sophia's loneliness ("I feel she knows about life"). When Catherine Oliphant quotes it during Tom's crisis of faith, she explains, "That isn't a comfortable poem [and] isn't meant to be. People have so many wrong ideas about the Victorians." The complexity of the Victorian mind is shown by the surprising popularity of 'Lead, Kindly Light' with its considerable ambiguity, doubt, and intellectual struggle. Their faith was not the simple opiate which we tend to patronize or envy.

Newman felt his poem too personal and melancholy for corporate singing. He was remarkably forbearing when hymnal editors tampered with his words to christianize and improve them: "Lead, Savior, Lead" was one of the more harmless versions. But it was not the song he called for when dying. Many of his contemporaries held it in higher esteem than he did. It captured the 19th-century imagination to a great degree *because* of its ambiguity and wistful longing for certainty. Queen Victoria recited the final stanza to her dying son the Duke of Albany, and requested it to be read in her own final hours. It was often used at seances; and at a World Parliament of Religions in 1895 the only two things on which all delegates could agree were the recitation of the Lord's Prayer and the singing of 'Lead, Kindly Light'. In January 1928 it was the one congregational hymn at the Westminster Abbey funeral service for the novelist and poet Thomas Hardy.

While living at the Coppice in 1943, Barbara read Cardinal Newman's autobiography and found its theology difficult. But, according to her diary, she [1]

> liked the account of how 'Lead, Kindly Light' came to be written. It was in 1833, when Newman was 32 [twelve years before his conversion to Rome. Like one of Harriet Bede's curates Newman had a fragile constitution.] ... After

a tour of Italy, during which he was ill of a fever, he waited for a ship home at Palermo for three weeks. At last [he] got off in an orange boat bound for Marseilles. [It was] becalmed a whole week in the Straits of Bonifacio. There it was that [he] wrote the lines Lead, Kindly Light.

In later years Newman claimed that the hymn's popularity was due to the romantic tune by Dr Dykes, and that he had forgotten what was meant by the enigmatic reference to "angel faces loved and lost". I suspect the saintly Cardinal was fibbing naughtily. The kindly light refers to the pillar of fire that led the Israelites through the wilderness. Whether the angel faces are departed relatives, old loves, outgrown certainties, or lost innocence remains unclear. But it is easy to see how text and tune fit Barbara's melancholy nostalgic mood after the end of her relationship with Gordon Glover. In that difficult time, she seems to have found comfort in using the phrase "One step enough for me" almost like a mantra. Thirty years later (in 1971) she wrote rather frostily, "It amuses me that Malcolm Muggeridge describes *Lead, Kindly Light* as 'exquisite.' *Not* quite the word". [2] However, the shamelessly romantic tune by Dr Dykes, the quintessential Victorian hymn composer, *might* be called exquisite.

Instead of detailing the abundance of hymn-references in Barbara's novels, I should like to focus on two more great Victorian hymnwriters, whose personalities seem to have appealed to other aspects of Barbara's imagination, for neither was as melancholy as Newman. In the marvelous book *Abide with Me: The World of Victorian Hymns*, Ian Bradley writes:[3]

> It is tempting to categorize Victorian women hymnwriters into two distinct types: the sickly spinster who pours her frustration into highly charged verse of an intensely emotional hue, and the robust and active wife and mother who writes with more objectivity and control.

I think this sentence would have amused Barbara, so we will have one hymnwriter of each type. They are almost the sort of characters who might show up in a Pym novel: Connie Aspinall being the emotional spinster who plays the harp (astonishing the villagers), and the bossy and formidable clergy-wife, Agatha Hoccleve.

First the sickly maiden-lady, Frances Ridley Havergal, daughter of a clergyman (1836-79). I find no explicit reference to her in the novels, but there are two significant ones in Barbara's diaries. In 1958 she describes a visit to her old friend from the Coppice, Honor Wyatt: [4]

> By my bed Honor has put *Memorials of Frances Ridley Havergal*. How almost enviable were the lives of those Victorian lady hymnwriters – the leisurely travel abroad, faith and purpose in life [note the contrast with Newman's uncertainty]. In her study [was] her American typewriter, her harp-piano at which she composed hymns. Somebody had given her 'A Journal of Mercies' in which every day she noted down the particular mercy she received.

Twenty years later there is a fascinating and heartbreaking diary entry written during Barbara's final illness. It explores the idea for a novel that was never to be written.

In this new novel there will be two women ... One from a privileged background, the other from a more ordinary one (but not working class) ... The great house where one lives becomes a hotel for conferences ... A hymnwriter in the family, a woman like Frances Ridley Havergal or Charlotte Elliott [who wrote *Just As I Am*, the invitation hymn at Billy Graham crusades]. When she comes to stay with her friend she hopes to 'get to know her husband better' – with unexpected results.[5]

There were no such frivolous romantic elements in the real life of Miss Havergal. The daughter of a clergyman, she packed a very full life into forty-three years. Rumors of her invalidism are somewhat exaggerated: swimming, backpacking in the Lake District, and mountain-climbing in Switzerland suggest that she would have made a good companion hiking with packed lunches over Exmoor. Frances was something of a child prodigy, possessed of lists the following accomplishments:[6]

She learned to read at age three; she read the Bible at age four; committed to memory the Psalms, Isaiah, the minor Prophets, and the entire New Testament; had a lovely voice and excellent keyboard skills; could play from memory all of Handel and much of Mendelssohn and Beethoven.

She grew up to be an ardent lay-evangelist. Well had she been named for Nicholas Ridley, the Reformation bishop burned at the stake by Mary Tudor. Here is an entry from Miss Havergal's diary:[7]

I went for a visit of five days to Arely House in Worcestershire. There were ten persons in the house, some unconverted and long prayed-for, some converted but not rejoicing Christians. I prayed, 'Lord, give me all in this house.' And he just did. Before I left the house everyone had got a blessing. The last night of my visit I was too happy to sleep, and little couplets composed themselves, chiming in my heart.

The great hymnologist Erik Routley concludes:[8]

Not all of us are sure that she might not have proved a somewhat overwhelming houseguest, but one must admire — even while keeping a safe distance — her zeal and sincerity. She was a facile writer, and sometimes she wrote doggerel.

However, Frances herself was modest about her literary gifts, attributing any success to its divine inspiration.[9]

Writing is praying with me, for I never write even a line by myself. I write like a little child who looks up at each sentence to ask, 'And what shall I say next?' That is just what I do".

Her hymns of personal devotion, such as *Take My Life and Let It Be*, are "permeated with the fragrance of her passionate love of Jesus," according to Victorian hymnologist John Julian.

Finally, we come to the gallant, cheerful clergy-wife, so admired by Jane Cleveland: Cecil Frances Alexander, known to her friends as Fanny. The daughter of an English military officer who socialized with the Anglo-Irish aristocracy, Fanny Humphreys achieved a significant literary reputation before she married at the age of thirty-two. Her *Hymns for Little Children* was a bestseller, with a preface by the scholarly John Keble and needing no less than one hundred editions in the second half of the 19th century. The Poet Laureate Alfred Tennyson admitted to being envious of her long poem "The Burial of Moses." She spent her literary proceeds for good works, such as founding a school for the deaf, and walked miles each day ministering to "the sick, the poor, and the hungry, regardless of creed."

When she wed The Reverend William Alexander, he seemed destined for an unpromising career. His Oxford days had been debt-ridden and academically disastrous, so he must have realized that (like John Challow) he needed an older and steadier woman to take him in hand. The excellence of his wife was undoubtedly a factor in his appointment as a bishop in 1867. It is sad that Fanny did not live to see him made Primate Archbishop of All Ireland in 1896. She died just three days before their 45th wedding anniversary.

Fanny is without peer as "the Queen of Children's Hymnody," although appreciation of her best hymns is not limited to the Sunday School. Ian Bradley writes:[10]

> While other women wrote to ... express in deeply personal and subjective terms their own relationship with God, Mrs Alexander sought simply to teach. Although her personal sympathies probably lay with moderate Anglo-Catholicism [at a time when divisions within the Anglican Church were keenly felt], there is no particular party feel to her hymns. They are for the most part a model of theological objectivity and simplicity in expounding the essential points of Christianity.

She is unfairly criticized for the text of "Within the churchyard, side by side, / Are many long low graves," which Mr Spears recalls when trying to avoid the cutting of the churchyard grass:*

> Not one they ever sang now; 'morbid'... Tom couldn't remember whether it was included in the English Hymnal, probably not; it had some questionable lines (FGL 142).

This was actually written with a practical didactic purpose in mind. Bradley explains:[11]

> Death was a much more common experience for Victorian children than it is for young people today.... [The graphic focus on death in Victorian hymnody, even in children's hymns] sprang from a sincere desire to make some sort of pastoral and theological sense out of a profoundly upsetting process which took so many children away from their siblings and parents.

Mrs Alexander said that "a namby-pamby, childish style is most unpleasing to children, especially to boys; it is surprising how soon they can understand and follow poetry of a high order".[12] This is no doubt the secret of the enduring excellence of her greatest works, which include *Once in Royal David's City* and *There is a Green Hill Far Away*.

But her most famous and finest hymn is undoubtedly "All Things Bright and Beautiful," the one sung at the undenominational service following the lecture at which Aylwin Forbes faints and Dulcie falls in love:

> A youngish woman, looking grimly determined, sat pedalling at the harmonium. Dulcie sang in a loud indignant voice, waiting for the lines 'the rich man in his castle, the poor man at his gate...' but they never came.
> Then she saw that the verse had been left out. She sat down, feeling cheated of her indignation. The lay reader then gave an address showing how all work can be done to the Glory of God, even making an index ... (NFR, 20).

As in any well-planned service, the theme of the hymn relates to that of the address, which speaks of the Glory of God. It is my opinion that God does not mind sharing his Glory with the creative artist, who "gives us eyes to see" things and has "the lips that tell." We hold the conviction that Barbara Pym is such an artist. We give thanks for her bright and beautiful world, all the truer for its bittersweet threads, and acknowledge that she "has done all things well"!

References

1. Barbara Pym, *A Very Private Eye*; Grafton Books, 1985; New York: E. P. Dutton, 1984. page 16, 11 Feb. 1943

2. Ibid, p. 261; 22 April 197

3. Bradley, Ian, *Abide with Me: The World of Victorian Hymns*, p. 91

4. Pym, Ibid, p. 199, 15 June 1969

5. Ibid, p. 329; 24 June 1979

6. *Companion to the Service Book and Hymnal*, ed. William A. Seaman (Minneapolis: Augsburg, 1976), 451.

7. *Baptist Hymnal Companion*, Revised Edition, ed. R.W. Thomson (London: Psalms and Hymns Trust, 1967), p. 288.

8. Erik Routley, *A Panorama of Christian Hymnody*, The Liturgical Press, 1979, p. 116.

9. Vincent Lenti, "Hymns for Little Children: The Life and Legacy of Cecil Frances Alexander," *The Hymn*, vol. 50 no. 3, July 1999.

10. Ian Bradley, *Abide with Me: The World of Victorian Hymns* (London: SCM Press, 1997), p. 95

11. Ibid, pp. 113-14

12. *The Baptist Hymn Book Companion* p. 131

* Within the churchyard, side by side,
Are many long low graves,
...And some have stones set over them,
On some the green grass waves.

Full many a little Christian child,
Woman and man lies there;
And we pass near them every time
When we go in to prayer.

They cannot hear our footsteps come,
They do not see us pass;
They cannot feel the warm bright sun,
That shines upon the grass.

They do not hear when the great bell
Is ringing overhead;
They cannot rise and come to Church
With us, for they are dead.

Works of Barbara Pym cited in the text, with editions and abbreviations used for the titles:

Crampton Hodnet Jonathan Cape, 1950; New York: E.P. Dutton, 1985; CH

Excellent Women 1949-51; London: Jonathan Cape, 1952; Pan Books, 1995; New York: Perennial Library, 1980; EW

A Few Green Leaves 1977-9; London: Flamingo, 1994. New York: Perennial, 1981; AFGL

A Glass of Blessings 1955-6; London: Pan Books in association with Jonathan Cape, 1994; New York: Perennial, 1981; AGOB.

Jane and Prudence 1950-2; London: Jonathan Cape, 1979; New York: Perennial, 1982; JAP

Less Than Angels 1953-4; London: Pan Books, 1993; New York: Perennial. 1982; LTA.

No Fond Return of Love 1957-60; London: Pan Books in association with Jonathan Cape, 1993; New York: Perennial, 1984; NFROL.

PYM MS The papers of Barbara Pym. Department of Western Manuscripts, Bodleian Library, Oxford. Cited in the text by manuscript and folio number.

Quartet in Autumn 1973-6; London: Flamingo, 1994; New York: Perennial. 1980; QIA.

Some Tame Gazelle 1934-50; London: Pan Books, 1993; New York: Perennial, 1984; STG.

The Sweet Dove Died 1963-9; London: Flamingo, 1994; New York: Perennial, 1980; TSDD.

An Unsuitable Attachment 1960-5; Ed. Hazel Holt. London: Pan Books in association with Jonathan Cape,1993; New York: Perennial, 1983; AUA.

A Very Private Eye: The Diaries, Letters and Notebooks of Barbara Pym. 1984. Ed. Hazel Holt and Hilary Pym. London: Macmillan, 1994; Grafton Books, 1985; New York: E. P. Dutton, 1984; AVPE.

Contributors

TRIONA ADAMS read English at St Hilda's College, Oxford. Upon leaving College she worked as a television researcher, then became an agent representing actors and directors. She is a contributor to *The New Dictionary of National Biography*. She attended her first Barbara Pym Conference whilst still a student at St Hilda's, and has given various papers to the Society.

"Clergy wives: Roman matrons and Christian martyrs" was presented at the Barbara Pym Society conference at St Hilda's, Oxford, 14-15 Sept. 1996

ELEONORE BIBER (M.A., Ph.D., University of Vienna), born and bred Viennese, is a member of the Barbara Pym Society. She has delivered papers on the novelist at gatherings of the Society and the English Speaking Union. She has taught English, German, comparative literature and drama at a grammar school in Vienna. Her research focuses on the modern Anglo-Catholic novel and Victorian literature of faith and doubt.

"A mini-history of Anglo-Catholicism " was presented at the Spring Meeting of the Barbara Pym Society, Holborn, 17 May 1998

"A strong smell of incense: aspects of Anglo-Catholicism in Pym's novels" was presented at the Barbara Pym Society of North America Conference, Harvard, 1 April 2001.

TIM BURNETT was born in 1937, and was educated at Eton and Trinity College, Cambridge. He served in the Coldstream Guards 1956-1958. He joined the Department of Manuscripts in the British Museum as an Assistant Keeper in 1961 and was Head of the Manuscript Department in what had become the British Library 1986-1997. In retirement he works for a firm of Fine Art Agents. Among his publications are: *The Rise and Fall of a Regency Dandy: The Life and Times of Scrope Berdmore Davies*, 1981; *Byron, Childe Harold Canto III*, facsimile edition, 1987; *Robert Browning, The Ring and the Book*, three volumes, 1998-2004, part of the OUP Oxford English Texts Edition of the *Poetical Works of Robert Browning*.

"Social class and the clergy" is an abbreviated version of the paper presented at the Barbara Pym Society North American conference, Boston, 30 March 2003

KATE CHARLES, a prominent crime writer, is a former Chairman of the Crime Writers' Association. Her interest in churches is central to her own novels, and has caused them to be reviewed as 'a blood-stained version of the world of Barbara Pym'. She is currently Chairman of the Barbara Pym Society.

"A mini-history of Anglo-Catholicism " was presented at the Spring Meeting of the Barbara Pym Society, Holborn, 17 May 1998

"At ease with ladies: Barbara Pym and the clergy" is an abbreviated version of the paper delivered at the North American Conference of the Barbara Pym Society, Cambridge, Mass., 29-30 March 2003

THE REVD. DAVID COCKERELL was Adult Education and Training Officer for the Diocese of Ely Cathedral, and is now a parish priest in the Ely Diocese.

"What relevance does the Church of Barbara Pym have to the world and Church of today?" was presented at the Barbara Pym Society conference at St Hilda's, Oxford, 14-15 Sept. 1996

JOY GRANT

"Birds, woodworm and Jesuits: Roman Catholicism in Barbara Pym's novels" was presented at the Barbara Pym Society conference at St Hilda's, Oxford, 14-15 Sept. 1996

THE REVEREND PREBENDARY GERARD IRVINE spent all of his distinguished career in parish ministry, with long incumbencies at St Cuthbert's Philbeach Gardens and St Matthew's Westminster in the Diocese of London. A friend and supporter of many literary figures of the 20th century, including Sir John Betjeman and Barbara Pym, he is now retired and living in Brighton.

"The Clerical Directory from the novels of Barbara Pym" was presented at the Barbara Pym Society conference at St Hilda's, Oxford, 14-15 Sept. 1996

JUDY B. McINNIS is Professor of Spanish at the University of Delaware with joint appointments in the programs of Comparative Literature, Women's Studies, and

Latin American Studies. Her first love was English Literature, which she continues to cultivate with occasional papers on English authors and an annual Study Abroad Theater Program to London.

"Communal rites: tea, wine and Milton in Barbara Pym's novels" was presented at the Barbara Pym Society conference at Cambridge, Mass, 29-30 March 2003; first appeared in *Renascence* 48.4, Summer 1996, pp 279-295

FATHER GABRIEL MYERS has been a monk of St Anselm's Abbey, Washington, DC, since 1987, where he serves as organist-choirmaster and teaches religion in the Abbey School.

"St Benedict in the Precinct: a Monkish view" is an abbreviated version of the paper presented at the Barbara Pym Society conference at St Hilda's, Oxford, 14-15 Sept. 1996

"Miss Pym and the Victorian hymn" was presented at the Barbara Pym Society of North America Conference, Harvard, 1 April 2001, and at Holborn, London, 9 June 2002

JAMES RUNCIE is a writer and film-maker. His film, *Miss Pym's Day Out,* with Patricia Routledge and Hilary Walton, was shown on BBC 2 in 1992, won a Royal Television Society Award and was shortlisted for a BAFTA. Since then he has made numerous films, including *Heaven, The Figure on the Cross, My Father,* (all three of which have won awards), *The Great Fire, Darwin's Daughter,* and *Saturday/Sunday.* His novels, *The Discovery of Chocolate* and *The Colour of Heaven* are published by Harper Collins, and he is currently at work on a third.

ROBERT SMITH was a close friend of Barbara Pym's, sharing her interest in Anglicanism and churches, who became Associate Professor of History at the University of Lagos.

"Exploring London churches with Barbara Pym" was presented to the Barbara Pym Society, London, April 1996

Index

'King of glory, king of peace' 96
'Lead kindly light' 100-101
Milton's 47
'New every morning' 21
'Within the churchyard' 103, 105

incense 20, 24-5, 32, 34, 75
International African Institute 5, 14
Irvine, Father Gerard 23, 108

James, Henry 90
Jane and Prudence 25, 28, 38, 40,
    51, 52, 59, 84-8, 89
    Barbara Bird 92
    church and social class 74
    clergy 61, 69-70
    hymns 99
    religious bookshop 29-30, 35
    tea 41
Jarvis, Father William 97
Jesuits 32
Julian, John 102

Keats, John 31
Keble, John 51, 103
    'New every morning' 21
Kirby, Fr. Marc-Daniel 98
Knox, Ronald 30, 32

Larkin, Philip 53, 90, 92
    'Church Going' 94
    'Toads Revisited' 97
Less than Angels 38, 41, 43-4, 52,
    89, 90
    Anglo-Catholicism 18, 20, 26-7
    Barnes 95
    clergy 33
Liddell, Robert 37, 77, 93, 95
    poem about Pym and Harvey 38
Little St Mary's Church, Cambridge
    75
London
    churches 14-16, 17, 24
    'Pym pilgrimage' 93-4
    see also place names
Long, Robert Emmett 86
love, sacred and profane 36-40, 44-8
love-making 44
Lowder, Charles 22

Mackenzie, Compton 23
martyrdom 77, 79, 81, 83, 84
Mass *see* Eucharist
McAteer, Fr. Sean 15
McInnis, Judy 108
Milton, John 36, 37-8, 41, 45, 46,
    47-8
    Of Church Dogma 41
    Paradise Lost 36, 37-8, 39, 40, 47
    Samson Agonistes 37, 38, 39, 40
monasteries 51-4, 89, 93
*Mowbray's Church Guide for
    Tourists* 18
Muggeridge, Malcolm 101
Myers, Fr. Gabriel 1, 108

names, significance of 45-6
Nardin, Jane 48
Newman, Cardinal John Henry 21,
    22, 51, 100-101
No Fond Return of Love
    Anglo-Catholicism 25, 27-8, 29-30,
    69-70
    anonymous author 92
    clergy 16, 56, 61, 63-4, 67
    research 91-2
    tea 41
    wine 43, 44
nuns 29, 34

Oates, Joyce Carol 93
Oxford 23, 96
    Pusey House 15
Oxford Movement 17, 20-2, 24, 29

Palgrave, Francis Turner 97-8
parables 7
Petrarch, Francesco 37, 42
Petrement, Simone 12
Pevsner, Nikolaus 15
Phelps, Gilbert 96
Pimlico, London 75
    St Gabriel's Church 14, 17, 24, 73,
    93-4
Plough Inn, Finstock, Oxfordshire
    96, 97
prayer 53-4, 89
prejudice 74-6
Protestant Trust Society 32
Protestantism 33, 41-2, 51